Landscapes of the

BASQUE COUNTRY

of Spain and France

a countryside guide

Philip Cooper

SUNFLOWER BOOKS

First edition © 2005
Sunflower Books™
PO Box 36160
London SW7 3WS, UK
www.sunflowerbooks.co.uk

Published in the USA by
Hunter Publishing Inc
130 Campus Drive
Edison, NJ 08818
www.hunterpublishing.com

ISBN 1-85691-276-0

Donostia — Peine de los Vientos

Important note to the reader

We have tried to ensure that the descriptions and maps in this book are error-free at press date. The book will be updated, where necessary, whenever future printings permit. It will be very helpful for us to receive your comments (sent in care of the publishers, please) for the updating of future printings.

We also rely on those who use this book — especially walkers — to take along a good supply of common sense when they explore. Conditions can change fairly rapidly in the Basque Country, and *storm damage or bulldozing may make a route unsafe at any time*. If the route is not as we outline it here, and your way ahead is not secure, return to the point of departure. *Never attempt to complete a tour or walk under hazardous conditions!* Please read carefully the notes on pages 52 to 61, as well as the introductory comments at the beginning of each tour and walk (regarding road conditions, equipment, grade, distances and time, etc). Explore *safely*, while at the same time respecting the beauty of the countryside.

Cover photograph: ascending Aitzkorri (Walk 5)
Title page: Laguardia (Car tour 5)

Photographs: Philip Cooper and Nini Olaizola
Maps: John Underwood, based on maps from various sources: see page 52.
A CIP catalogue record for this book is available from the British Library.
Printed and bound in Spain by Grafo Industrias Gráficas, Basauri

10 9 8 7 6 5 4 3 2 1

❁ Contents

4   Landscapes of the Basque Country

● Preface

The Basque Country — Euskal Herria or Euskadi — can be defined in several ways. This book covers seven provinces forming a fairly homogeneous region in terms of language, culture and traditions. The Basque language — Euskera — is spoken to a greater or lesser extent in all these provinces, and is now widespread on road signs and maps, etc. For this reason Euskera names have been used in this book, together with their hitherto more common Spanish or French names as appropriate.

In Spain, the Basque Autonomous Community — la Comunidad Autónoma Vasca or C.A.V. for short — comprises the three provinces of Gipuzkoa (Guipúzcoa), Bizkaia (Vizcaya) and Araba (Alava). A fourth province, Nafarroa (Navarra) has separate autonomous status. The other three provinces, on the French side — Lapurdi (Labourd), Behe Nafarroa (Basse Navarre) and Xiberoa (Soule) collectively make up Iparralde ('the north side'). They do not have separate *département* status, since they form part of the Département des Pyrenées-Atlantiques, but nonetheless they share a common language, culture and tradition with the four provinces on the Spanish side. The total population of the seven provinces is around three million, about 260,000 of whom live in Iparralde.

Collectively the region presents a varied palette of landscapes and architectural styles, and this guide offers the chance to get to know some of the most beautiful corners of each province — areas which are only now starting to be discovered by non-locals as unspoilt travel destinations. The entire Basque coast from Biarritz to beyond Bilbao is mostly very rugged, with many thriving fishing towns and villages, plus the added attraction of some beautiful beach resorts, among which the most renowned is Donostia-San Sebastián, an excellent base for touring the region. All of Gipuzkoa and Bizkaia and northern Nafarroa, from the Baztán Valley eastwards towards the Pyrenees, are mountainous and have lush green countryside, in stark contrast to the drier plains of southern Nafarroa and Araba around and to the south of the provincial capitals of Iruña-Pamplona and Vitoria-Gasteiz respectively; these areas have more in common with parts of neighbouring Castile to the south, both geographically and to a certain extent culturally too. The main pilgrims' route to

Santiago passes through here by way of an added attraction. The French side is characterized by unspoilt picture-postcard inland villages and the more abrupt, dramatic mountain scenery of the north side of the Pyrenees, most spectacularly so in the canyon area of Xiberoa.

Historically, the origins of the Basque race and language continue to be open to debate. Archaeological finds — above all skull fragments of late Cro-Magnon man, and the similarity to present-day skull shape — lend weight to the theory that the region may have been continuously inhabited since Palaeolithic times, pre-dating the Indo-European invasions. Another attraction on walks in the region is the huge number of bronze and iron age burial sites in the form of dolmens and cromlechs.

It is said that the Basque Country was one of the last places to become urbanized in Europe, and the traditional Basque farmhouse or *caserío* (*baserri* in Euskera) remains an important focal point of Basque rural life today. One of the classic images one sees when touring through the region is the pastoral green valley with half-timbered or sturdy stone *baserri* dotted over the limestone rock hillsides. The very strong family unit, based on a traditional matriarchal society, would be centred on these places, and at times in the past, most notably during the Franco era, when Euskera was banned, use of the language was mainly confined to them. Verse-improvisation in Euskera as practised by *bertsolariak* originally developed in *baserri* and would play a key role in the language's survival and evolution.

This guide, while by no means being exhaustive, provides a series of car tours which in general follow minor scenic roads, off the beaten track wherever possible, to include many of the region's finest landscapes. There are 32 walks which include ascents of some of the best known peaks such as Mounts Txindoki, Anboto and Aitzkorri. These do not always follow the classic route, but rather one which is perhaps more beautiful and varied. Other walks include some of the best stretches of the Basque coast of Gipuzkoa, Bizkaia and Lapurdi, and some of the region's most beautiful forested areas, together with rivers, caves and canyons. There are also 19 relatively short walks for motorists which may be combined with the different car tours and are of a maximum of around 2 hours' duration.

The Basques are keen walkers themselves, and some of the better known routes can be well trodden at weekends, although all provide wonderful opportunities to get to know this beautiful and as yet relatively unspoilt region.

Acknowledgements

First and foremost I am indebted to my partner Nini Olaizola, who has provided me with the emotional support and encouragement to complete this project, accompanied me on most of the walks, taken many of the photographs and helped out enormously with the maps. I would then like to thank the people from the relevant tourist offices throughout the region who gave me many ideas and suggestions. A special thanks also to Iñaki Garmendia Barrena from the Departamento de Ordenación del Territorio Vasco y Medio Ambiente of the Basque Government in Vitoria-Gasteiz, Mark Wilson for providing good company on some of these and many other walks in the Basque Country over the years, and my daughter Sara for giving me constant inspiration in everything I do.

Useful books

This book focuses on an exploration of the countryside in the Basque region, and as such may be used in conjunction with a general guide such as the Rough Guides to the Pyrenees, Spain or France. For general background reading, the following are recommended:

Kurlansky, Mark (1999); *The Basque History of the World* (Vintage): an extremely informative book on all things Basque; very good background reading

Hooper, John (1995); *The New Spaniards* (Penguin Books Ltd.); interesting section on Basques and the Basque Country

Crane, Nicholas (1997); *Clear Waters Rising* (Penguin Books Ltd.); a walk across Europe from Cape Finisterre to Istanbul, passing through the Basque Country

The Center for Basque Studies at the University of Nevada, Reno, USA (http://basque.unr.edu), publishes a wide range of books in English on different subjects relating to Basques and the Basque Country. Among those of interest are:

Lasagabaster, Jesús María (1990); *Contemporary Basque Fiction. An Anthology*.

Aulestia, Gorka (2000); *The Basque Poetic Tradition*

Busca Isasi, José María (1993); *Traditional Basque Cooking. History and Preparation*.

Watson, Cameron (2003); *Modern Basque History. 18th century to the present.*

Finally, if you will be spending most of your time in the Pyrenees and travelling outside the Basque Country, you may wish to have the following guide from the same series:

Jenner, Paul, and Christine Smith (2005); *Landscapes of the Pyrenees* (Sunflower Books), which covers the entire range.

Short walks and picnic suggestions

Within the eight car tours described, there are 19 **short walks** of maximum 2h15min duration which are relatively easy, involving minimal climbing. These have been selected to provide a cross-section of different landscapes and are ideal for motorists who wish to explore some beautiful corners of the region without requiring any hiking experience. (Among the longer main walks described, there are also shorter options which follow part of the longer route; details are given in the introduction to each walk.)

Some of the short walks described in the car tours include well-known beauty spots and so may be quite busy in high season; others, for instance those visiting picnic sites, are simply some of my favourite spots — convenient stopping-off points on car tours, where it is worthwhile parking the car and setting off on foot.

There are unlimited options for **picnicking** throughout the Basque Country. The area is largely mountainous and forested, and many areas have been set aside for such a purpose. These may sometimes consist of just a couple of wooden benches beside a river, while others may have barbecue facilities and flush toilets.

I have called attention to some of my favourite picnic spots; these are mentioned in the introduction to each tour. There are also picnic spots along many of the main walks, and these are highlighted on the walking maps by the symbol (*P*) printed in green. Otherwise, to find picnic sites in general, look for signs indicating *merendero*, *pique-nique* or *atseden-lekua*.

When stocking up on supplies for picnics and walks, note that even small villages in the Spanish Basque Country usually have a bar where you can ask for substantial *bocadillos/bokatas* — ideal walkers' fare. Among the most common fillings for these sandwiches are different *tortillas* (omelettes), cheese, ham and chorizo. The Basque Country in general is renowned for its cuisine, and Basques take their eating very seriously indeed. The *sociedades gastronómicas* (gastronomic societies) constitute an important part of social life in the Spanish Basque provinces, where friends and family get together to

8

prepare classic dishes to perfection, and the *tapas* tradition (always referred to as *pintxos* in the Basque Country) is one to be savoured, with the best variety being available in coastal towns. Traditional markets are also excellent sources of fresh produce on both sides of the border. Another option is to look out for signs showing *baserriko produktoak* — farmhouse products — obtainable directly from farms along the way. In the French Basque Country, the best bet is to stock up on supplies either from supermarkets or village bakeries and small food shops, although many farms also sell their produce direct to the public. Look out in particular for signs indicating *ardi gasna* (sheep's cheese) throughout inland Iparralde.

Start of Walk 8 outside Etxalar

Touring

The Basque Country is an excellent centre for touring, as the landscapes are very varied and the distances relatively short. Roads are in the main in good condition, although often winding and narrow with much of the terrain being so mountainous.

The eight car tours described, while not covering every corner of the region, have been selected to offer a decent cross-section of different landscapes, as well as architectural and historical highlights, enabling the visitor to explore some of the most beautiful coastal and inland areas. All car tours give details of picnic sites, and also link up conveniently with the short walks for motorists and the longer walking routes.

The tours avoid main roads wherever possible, although some short stretches may be covered by dual carriageway or motorway if the alternative would entail driving through the centre of busy, congested towns. By and large, however, the tours follow the most scenic routes, at times quite off the beaten track. In fact, once away from the more popular coastal resorts, most of the Basque Country is waiting to be discovered!

Six of the car tours are circuits starting and finishing in the main provincial capitals of the region. Tours 1 and 2 start from Donostia-San Sebastián, justifiably the Spanish Basque Country's prime tourist destination with its fabulous beaches and very much the epicentre of all things Basque, culturally-speaking. Tour 3 is based around Bilbao, the region's largest and most dynamic city and former industrial giant which has been put on the map in recent years in particular by the Guggenheim Museum.

Tour 6 starts and finishes in Iruña-Pamplona, renowned for its *encierro* — the running of the bulls — during the fiestas of *San Fermines*. The city is steeped in history and is the capital of the immensely varied province of Nafarroa, the largest of the seven provinces covered in this book.

Tours 7 (from Bayonne/Baiona) and 8 (from St Jean-Pied-de-Port/Donibane Garazi) include many of the most beautiful corners of Iparralde, the French Basque Country. The French Basque coast makes another fine touring centre, with the famed resorts of Biarritz and St Jean-de-Luz/Donibane Lohizun being ideal bases from which to explore both the coast itself and the unspoilt hinterland of the

Pyrenean foothills and higher peaks of the canyon country of Xiberoa.

Tours 4 and 5 are somewhat different in that they have been designed as one-way routes between major centres, to enable the visitor to cover a larger area and link up with the other car tours. These tours converge in Vitoria-Gasteiz, the elegant yet relatively off-the-beaten-track administrative capital of the *Comunidad Autónoma Vasca* and the city in Spain with the most green spaces per inhabitant. Tour 4 follows some of the least-known yet most picturesque corners of southern Bizkaia and Western Araba, using Bilbao as a starting point. Tour 5 covers the Rioja Alavesa wine-growing country and the sierras of Toloño-Cantabria, Kodes, Urbasa and Aralar, terminating in Iruña-Pamplona.

Needless to say, all eight tours, although designed to be completed in the time estimated, can easily be extended over several days, especially taking into account the wide range of accommodation options available in even the most rural of areas. Note that driving times given do not make allowances for more than the briefest of stops!

Lack of space makes it impossible to include town/city plans, but precise directions are in any case given for leaving towns and cities.

The large touring map is designed to be held out opposite the touring notes and contains all the information you need to follow the tours suggested. **Symbols** for various amenities are printed in the text but only shown on the map for the more remote locations; any reasonably-sized town will have petrol, restaurants, and accommodation, etc.

Should you wish to buy **more detailed maps**, there are a couple of very useful ones covering the whole region. Two maps which cover all areas included in this book are the Firestone R-2 1:200 000 map of *Navarra, País Vasco and Rioja*, especially useful if travelling to neighbouring regions and on sale in local petrol stations, and the 1:250 000 *mapa turístico de Euskal Herria* which is available from bookshops and kiosks throughout the region. Also worth considering is the 1:200 000 Firestone T-33 map of the Pyrenees, incorporating Car tours 2, 6, 7 and 8.

Regarding **weather conditions**: the Pyrenean sections of Car tours 6 and 8 in Nafarroa and Xiberoa and, to a lesser extent, the routes through the sierras visited on Car tours 4 and 5 may well be snow-covered in mid-winter, meaning that some of the more minor roads might be temporarily closed until the snow plough can get through. In all other cases, roads would normally be open all year round.

Car tour 1: THE VERDANT VALLEYS, MOUNTAINS AND WILD COASTAL SCENERY OF GIPUZKOA

Donostia-San Sebastián • Tolosa • Larraitz • Ordizia • Errezil • Azpeitia • Loiola • Azkoitia • Madariaga • Lastur valley • Zumaia • Getaria • Zarautz • Orio • Donostia-San Sebastián

159km/98mi; about 4h driving time
En route: Short walks for motorists 1 and 2; Walks 1, 2, 3, 4 and 5
Picnic suggestions: in Donostia-San Sebastián itself, either near the top of **Mt Urgull** or on **Santa**

Clara island (0km), **Larraitz** (40km); **Beunde** near the start of Walk 5 to Aitzkorri (a 21km detour from Ordizia at the 49km-point); **Aittola** (101km); **Ratón de San Antón**, Getaria (131km)

This tour covers much of the best mountain and coastal scenery of Gipuzkoa. The province is extremely green and mountainous, and some of the classic hill walks in the region are on or near our route. The beautiful, tranquil valleys of Errezil and Lastur provide a marked contrast to the rugged coastline with its colourful fishing villages.

Donostia-San Sebastián★
(✳⚓🏔✕🍴🅿🖼M) is an attractive seaside resort with a colourful harbour and a lively old town filled with bars offering the most succulent *pintxos*. Other focal points are the San Telmo Museum, the Aquarium and **Mt Urgull** (🎠P) and its fortifications. Many paths lead up this hill, from where there are great views over the city and out to sea; an excellent picnic spot is just below the Christ statue at the top. The city also boasts three good beaches. The main one — the perfect horseshoe bay of **La Concha** — looks out to **Santa Clara Island** (🎠P), which is another great place to picnic and spend the day in summer. Walk 1, to the Faro de la Plata (lighthouse), starts from the tourist office on Calle Reina Regente 3.
From the Pio XII roundabout by the bus station, follow signs for VITORIA-GASTEIZ on the N1, heading down the fairly industrial **Oria Valley** via **Andoain**★ and **Tolosa** (23km ⚓✕🍴🅿), famous

for its riotous week-long carnival held around the end of February each year. Soon after Tolosa, at JUNCTION 431, turn off the main road to **Alegia** (28km ✕🍴). Follow signs into the village and when you reach a small car park beside the railway station, take an unmarked street to the left, down through the village proper and across the river bridge. Immediately after the bridge, turn right along the river and up the hill on the GI3670, signposted towards ABALTZISKETA. This fairly narrow road climbs up through the forest until it reaches the ridge-top (35km) from where the spectacular views begin. Directly in front of you is the abrupt north face of the **Sierra de Aralar** and far below to the right the Oria Valley with the mountains of central Gipuzkoa beyond. Along the route there are numerous *baserri* and, on the ridge itself, a couple of wonderfully located hilltop villages. The main one is **Abaltzisketa** (39km ✝🏔🖼), where the Church of John the Baptist contains one of the most interesting Romanesque-Gothic porticos in the province. From

Detours: from Andoain you can take a detour to the start of Walk 2 at Besabi or Walk 3 at Alkiza.

12

Errezil village

here on, the impressive 'Matterhorn' of **Mt Txindoki** looms directly ahead, at the far end of the Sierra de Aralar (photograph page 56). The sierra ends at **Larraitz** (40km ✳🏔✕📷🅿), just a couple of houses and rustic bars, with a nice, shady picnic site. This is the starting point for Walk 4 to Txindoki.

Follow the winding road down through **Zaldibia** (46km 🏔✕), with great views of the south face of Txindoki to the left and its smaller neighbouring mountain, **Gaztelu**, slightly further to the right. On reaching the main road at the first roundabout in **Ordizia** (49km ✕🅿) — where the traditional Wednesday morning farmers' market in the main square is the best in the province — turn right towards DONOSTIA-SAN SEBASTIAN, rejoining the N1.

(Or, to get to the start of Walk 5, turn *left* here towards VITORIA-GASTEIZ and see the access notes on page 72.)

The main tour now loops back past **Alegia** to the next junction, JUNCTION 433 (61km), and onto the GI2634 towards AZPEITIA. Turn sharp left almost immediately on a narrow road which follows the river. This leads to **Albistur** (🏔✕) in the valley to the right, where there are a couple of small bars/restaurants renowned for their high quality red Tolosa beans, served with cabbage and chorizo — hearty walkers' fare. As the road climbs, the views of this valley become increasingly impressive, flanked by the limestone form of **Mt Ernio** to the right.

Continue over the **Bidania Pass** (510m) and through the village of **Bidegoian** (🏔), the highest in Gipuzkoa. At the main fork in the village (70km), veer right towards ERREZIL and AZPEITIA. Just after the

Iturburu Pass (550m) the road passes under a bridge, and before us is the **Balcón de Gipuzkoa** (📷), high above the lush green **Errezil Valley** (✳). This is one of the classic Basque landscapes — with sheep grazing on the hillsides, scattered *baserri* and the beautiful village of Errezil below.

Descend to the village of **Errezil** (75km ♨🏔✕), dominated by the church of St Martin de Tours — dating back to the early Middle Ages and worth a visit for its huge wood carving of St Martin on horseback. From Errezil move on to the important furniture-making town of **Azpeitia** (85k ♨🏔✕🅿) at the bottom of the valley, overlooked by the **Izarraitz Massif**; the highest peak in the range, **Erlo** (1026m), rises directly above the town.

At the first roundabout, turn left and follow the signs towards AZKOITIA on the GI131. You circle round Azpeitia and follow a tree-lined avenue past the 17th-century **Basilica of San Ignacio de Loiola** (89km ♨⛰✕), the birthplace of the founder of the Jesuit movement. Continue on to the first roundabout just before **Azkoitia**, where you take the second right turn towards ELGOIBAR. Follow this main road, which flanks **Mt Xoxote** (906m), the lower peak of the Izarraitz Massif, crowned by a huge statue of San Ignacio de Loiola. At a junction, turn right towards AZKARATE PASS and MADARIAGA. From **Azkarate Pass** take the road which veers sharply to the right and narrows as it passes through

13

Short walk for motorists

🚗 1 **Lastur valley circuit**
5km/3mi; 1h40min. This circuit provides a good overview of the valley's charms, as you follow the remnants of an old water channel through the forest and back along the valley floor. At the beginning there is a fairly steep ascent of 400m from the village up into the forest, from where the path is almost completely on the flat before descending to the valley floor and returning on the road.

Opposite the village square in **Lastur**, take the yellow and white waymarked path (signposted DEBA) which climbs quite steeply behind the *frontón* up into the pine forest. When a white *baserri* comes into view on your right and the path levels out, turn left and go through a **gate (15min)**. You enter a pine forest and follow an old trail beside a water channel, with glimpses of the valley down through the trees. Pine gives way to oak and, after you go through a **turnstile (30min)**, moss-covered limestone increasingly invades the somewhat narrow (but perfectly safe) trail.

Take the upper path to the left (still waymarked), soon leaving the forest and enjoying clear views of the valley's karst landscape. On reaching a large beech tree, a gravel path heads up the hill towards Mt Arbil (signposted; **45min)**.

Ignore this and make for the **Arrasketa** *baserri*, diagonally below to the left. The property itself is beautifully located above the valley and opposite is a huge, centuries-old holm oak. Descend an asphalted lane to the **valley floor (1h)** and return along the road, which is usually pleasantly traffic-free — affording a closer look at the pastoral surroundings as you return to the village square in **Lastur (1h40min)**.

the hamlet of **Madariaga** and winds through an extensive pine forest. The small Bar Otarre (99km ✕☎) on the left, with an ornate garden and benches outside, makes a very pleasant place to stop and view the valley and surrounding mountains. Alternatively, press on for another 2km along this highly scenic road to a car park and the small **Aittola picnic site** (101km ⇤P). This beautiful stretch of road meanders along the ridgetop for a while, with views down to a rocky gorge to the right.

(*Detour:* Just 1km further on, a road to the right leads to AITTOLA ZAR. The road drops steeply into the **Goltzibar Gorge** and **Aittola Zar** (✳🏠✕), a *baserri* perched just above it. This remote *venta* (inn) is several hundreds years old and, although it has now been refurbished, it retains its charm.) On the main route, exercise special caution on the sharp bends as the road descends into the **Lastur valley**. Once down in the valley, turn left to the hamlet of **Lastur** (109km ✳🏠✕🚗1). This is a beautiful valley, only marginally spoilt at the beginning by the eyesore of a fairly large quarry; otherwise, Lastur and its surroundings have a forgotten, edge-of-the-world feeling about them. The village itself consists of an old church, a fully operational water mill making corn flour for delicious *talo* bread (on sale in the shop by the bar), a couple of half-timbered houses, a cosy little bar serving food and the whole main square serving as a rustic bullring that has been used for such purpose for centuries. Four or five young bulls (*novillos*) are still let loose at weekends. The karst scenery throughout this valley is well worth exploring, preferably on foot from the village square. From Lastur, return to the crossroads (110km) and turn left

Water mill at Lastur

to **Itziar** (115km 🚉) on the main N634 Bilbao-San Sebastián road. Descend to the coast and the busy, attractive fishing town of **Zumaia** (125km 🛉🏔🏨✕🚉M) at the mouth of the **Urola River**. There are good beaches and interesting cliff formations just a few hundred metres west of the town, which is very popular in summer with locals. The main road crosses the river once beyond the town and passes the house-museum of the Basque painter Zuloaga on the left (open Easter-15/09; Wed-Sun 16.00-20.00). The route hugs the coast as the Ratón de San Antón — the mouse-shaped hill jutting out to sea at Getaria — comes into view. This is one of the most dramatic stretches of road on the Basque coast, and the waves often crash over, occasionally breaking the sea wall and requiring a rather tortuous detour inland via Meagas. **Getaria** (131km ✳🛉🏔🏨✕📷🚗2) is another colourful fishing village, dominated by the 15th-century Gothic church of San Salvador, curiously built right over the tunnel of the main street. There are many high-quality fish restaurants here. Juan Sebastián Elcano, the Basque seaman who captained Magellan's ship *Victoria* back to Spain after the latter's

untimely death in the Philippines, was born here, and there is a large memorial to him on the main road. From the harbour, the **Ratón de San Antón** makes a delightful spot for a picnic (🚏*P*), and there is a maze of paths snaking up to and around the lighthouse at the tip of the hill. More wild coastal scenery accompanies us as we head into **Zarautz** (134km 🏔🏨△✕🚉), a popular surfing and seaside resort with a beautiful long sandy beach. Continue through the town centre, past the motorway entrance to the right. Our route proceeds up the hill, still on the N634, and on to the next village of **Orio** (141km 🏨△✕), built alongside the **Oria River** estuary, where there are more of those colourful Basque fishing boats moored by the quayside. Cross the long river bridge into town and take the first left turn, signposted HONDARTZA and UDAL-CAMPING. Follow the road around the one-way system, along the main street and out of town for barely 1 km, until you pass under the motorway bridge. Follow the sign for IGELDO immediately afterwards and then take the next left (same signposting). This fairly narrow road soon reaches the ridgetop (146km), offering great views down to the sea. There are some rustic bars serving food along the top, and some picnic tables (150km 🚏*P*) to the left of the road. Pass the large Garoa camp site (△) and bypass Igeldo village (🏨), before descending towards the city via **Ondarreta Beach** and the **Antiguo** district. Following the one-way system, turn left towards CENTRO and drive around the famous **Concha Bay**. Turn right into CALLE URBIETA in the city centre, to return to our starting point at Pio XII in **Donostia-San Sebastián** (159km).

Getaria and the Ratón de San Antón from San Prudentzio's vineyards

Short walk for motorists

🚗 **2 Txakoli vineyards**

5km/3mi; 1h50min. This circuit in part follows an old cobbled path that originally formed part of a coastal branch of the Pilgrims' Route to Santiago known as the 'Calzada de la Costa.' Most of the route meanders through txakoli *vineyards — txakoli is a very dry, acidic sparkling white wine produced in just a few villages along this coast. It is served in any bar in the area. There is a short (50m) climb at the beginning of the path and about 250m of steady ascent up to the hamlet of Askizu, but overall this is a very easy circuit.*

From the roundabout at the entrance to **Getaria**, take the road up the hill (signposted to MEAGAS). After about 150m, turn right uphill on an attractive cobbled trail. Almost immediately to your right is the **first vineyard**. On reaching a roundabout (**5min**), the trail continues beside a large house called **Akerregi-Txiki**. This is the best-preserved section of the *calzada*, meandering up and down through the vineyards. When you join a road, follow it past the turning for San Prudentzio and down the hill. Then take a small lane to the left, past a very **old green- and white-painted house** (**30min**). The lane winds up to the hilltop

16

hamlet of **Askizu** (**45min**), with its imposing Gothic church. From the square, which has a decent map showing various walks in the area, follow the road to the right, out of the village. Soon you can see the breakwater of the port of Zumaia and its beach below. Take the second asphalted lane to the left, past some large **greenhouses** and, at the end, descend on an initially muddy and subsequently grassy path, keeping the sea directly in front of you. Before reaching the coast road, turn right and go through a **gate** (**1h05min**), along a scenic path parallel to the clifftops — with the vineyards now to your right. Just after passing through a small oak grove you come upon a very old *baserri* called **Bizkarraga** (**1h15min**), from where there is a fantastic view of the Ratón de San Antón.

The lane turns right, to **San Prudentzio** (**1h25min**), with a Romanesque chapel (key available in the hostal San Prudentzio) and two bars with nice terraces — the ideal place to rest and sample *txakoli*. Keep straight on to the crossroads, then turn left back along the road towards Getaria, returning on the same cobbled trail to the **Getaria** roundabout (**1h50min**).

Car tour 2: THE BAZTAN VALLEY OF NORTHERN NAFARROA AND PYRENEAN FOOTHILLS

Donostia-San Sebastián • Aiako Harria Parke Naturala • Lesaka • Etxalar • Zugarramurdi • Señorío de Bertiz Gardens • Doneztebe/Santesteban • Ituren • Zubieta • Goizueta • Donostia-San Sebastián

182km/113mi; about 4h30min driving time

En route: Short walk for motorists 3; Walks 6, 7, 8, 9, 10

Picnic suggestions: Collado de Uzpuru (a 12km detour from Oiartzun motorway turn-off at the 9km-point, on the way to the start of Walk 6); **Aritxulegi Tunnel** (21km); **Otsondo Pass** (78km); **Señorío de Bertiz Gardens** (105km); **Embalse de Mendaur** (a 5km detour from Aurtitz at the 116km-point); **Ugaldetxo,** beside the **Urumea River** (165km)

This tour offers the opportunity to visit some of the best-kept and most beautiful villages of Nafarroa in the picturesque Baztán Valley region. In olden times this was a land of nobles, evidence of which remains in the form of the many *casas-torre* (fortified houses) in the area. The tour also includes the fascinating area around Zugarramurdi (famous for its caves and the scene of many witch trials during the Inquisition) and the Aiako Harria Nature Reserve, the area around one of the Basque Country's most striking mountains bearing the same name.

For more details about **Donostia-San Sebastián**, see page 12 (Car tour 1). From Pio XII roundabout by the bus station, follow the motorway signs to IRUN-FRANCIA and turn off at JUNCTION 3 for OIARTZUN (9km). Turn left at the roundabout (but go *right* here, to get to the start of Walk 6 or to picnic at the Collado de Uzpuru).

The main tour takes the first right turn under the bridge, to **Oiartzun.** Just beyond the village, turn right (12km) on the GI3420 for LESAKA. Go through the village of **Ergoien** (14km 🏠 ✕), where there are several excellent rustic places to eat at very reasonable prices. The road heads straight towards the vertical rock face of

Embalse de San Antón

Short walk for motorists

🚗 3 The 'witches' trail'
6km/3.7mi; 2h. This mostly cobbled trail runs through caves and connects the village of Zugarramurdi with the Sara Caves in the French Basque Country. (The walk may be done in reverse from the Sara Caves during Car tour 7.) Allow an extra 30min to visit the Zugarramurdi Caves themselves. Entrance: € 2.50 adults; € 1 children; open 09.00-21.00 in summer, 09.00 till dusk the rest of the year. The Sara Caves are a more organized attraction with son-et-lumière *guided tours (€ 6 adults; € 3 children; open 10.00-19.00). The path is well waymarked in green and white.*
From the main square in **Zugarramurdi**, go down the lane opposite the church (sign: CUEVA/LEZEAK). Take the next left turn, past some beautiful old *baserri*, three of them converted into *landa etxeak*. Pass the entrance to the caves, on the left (**10min**), and continue to the end of the unsurfaced road. Then join the trail (signposted SARAKO LEZEAK). It plunges down into the verdant forest and crosses a rickety old wooden bridge beside **Infernuko Zubia** (Devil's Bridge; **15min**) over the **Infernuko Erreka** (Devil's Stream; the stream emerging from the cave). The cobbles then rise to a gravel road beside a stone house (**25min**). You rejoin the path, to the right, by some curious **'talking' stones** (**30min**), and descend to another cave, furnished with tables from the adjacent **Errotazarreko borda** bar (**40min**). The trail now runs alongside a lane all the way to a quarry just above the **Sarako Lezeak** (Sara Caves; **50min**). When the trail ends, go straight ahead down the road to the cave entrance (**55min**).
Retracing your steps to **Zugarramurdi** (**2h**) involves slightly more uphill walking.

Aiako Harriak (Peñas de Aia), and starts climbing as it enters the **Aiako Harria Parke Naturala** (17km ⚘), a protected area around the mountain. The border with Nafarroa is reached at the **Aritxulegi Tunnel** (439m; 21km ✗🅿️🚐P), where there is a refuge with bar/restaurant and a pleasant picnic site above the tunnel — just where Walk 7 begins.
Descend to the **San Antón Reservoir** (25km) and go on to **Agina** (30km 🚻), where there are a couple of **dolmens** close to the road. From here a short, 10-minute walk to the right (following the waymarked track towards BIANDITZ) leads to the hilltop site of **Aita-Donostia** (🅿️), one of the best known works by the Basque sculptor Oteiza, a good vantage point from which to view Aiako Harriak.
An extremely winding descent brings us to our first main stop in Baztán, **Lesaka** (39km 🚻🏨🏔️🏠 ✗🚗). Take the time to stroll along the river through the village; focal points are the Zabaleta *casa-torre*, one of the most impressive of its kind in the region, and the imposing 16th-century Gothic church of San Martín de Tours just above the village, accessed via a pretty cobbled alleyway. From Lesaka follow signs towards IRUÑA-PAMPLONA and turn right on the main N121-A (41km), following the **Bidasoa River** to the **Venta de Etxalar**. Then turn left to **Etxalar** (46km 🚻🏠✗), one of the most beautiful Baztán villages. The church graveyard has a fine collection of discoidal headstones and the village houses boast some of the most colourful wood-beamed façades in the area.
From Etxalar take the road to the right, past the church, signposted to ZUGARRAMURDI. Soon after leaving the village the road crosses the river and passes a collection of

Etxalar: church and discoidal headstones

baserri (48km). Walk 8 begins here. Then the road narrows and winds its way through an especially verdant section of hill country to the **Ibañeta Pass**. A large stone monolith marks the top of pass and a short, steep descent brings us to the village square of **Zugarramurdi** (64km ✳⛪✕∩⛟3). This was a major centre of witch trials during the Inquisition. In the immediate vicinity are three sets of **caves**. The caves at Zugarramurdi itself are the most impressive — their centrepiece is a huge natural arch through which a stream flows — purportedly the site of many an *akelerre* (witches' coven) in the past.

From the village square by the **church**, turn right, following signs towards DANTXARINEA and then a minor lane (66km) signed CUEVAS DE URDAX. Continue past the **Ikaburua Caves** (67km ∩) and take the next left turn. (***Detour:*** A 1km detour to the right here would take you to the attractive village of Urdazubi/Urdax (✝⛪✕∩) itself, site of the 11th-century Monastery of San Salvador and birthplace of Pedro Axular, who wrote the first texts in the Basque language.)

When you reach the main NA121 road, turn right towards IRUÑA-PAMPLONA. The road climbs to the **Otsondo Pass** (602m; 78km ⛩***P***), where there is an excellent picnic site to the right, and then descends towards the heart of the Baztán Valley proper. (***Detour:*** At 83km you might like to take another short detour to the left, to the one-street walled village of Amaiur (⛪),which is entered via a beautifully preserved gateway.)

The main tour keeps straight on, then takes the next left turn, the NA2600 towards ERRATZU (87km). You pass the small **Ordoki Distillery** on the right (look for the 'Licores Baztán' sign outside), where a variety of local fruit liquors are made. At the hamlet of **Bozate** there is an interesting *casa-torre* to the left, once owned by the *conquistador* Pedro Uxua. To get to Walk 9, continue straight on to the beautiful old village of Erratzu (⛪✕).

The main tour leaves Bozate by heading southwest. Follow signs to **Arizkun** (90km ⛪✕) and back to the main NA121. Turn left to **Elizondo** (95km ⛰⛪△✕⛽), the largest town in the valley, with more traditional Baztán architecture, especially alongside the river. Beyond Elizondo, leave the main road (103km) which bypasses a couple of villages. Instead, take the old NA121 to **Oronoz-Mugarri** (✕⛽). Just

Left: house in Zugarramurdi; above: houses at Etxalar

after the crossroads, the **Señorío de Bertiz Gardens** (105km ❀☂P) are to the right — another pleasant shady stop. Apart from the gardens themselves (entry fee), there is a picnic site to the left of the entrance and various waymarked paths in the woods around the gardens (details available from the tourist office by the picnic site).

Continuing on the NA121 towards IRUN, turn left on the NA170 to **Doneztebe/Santesteban** (110km ▲▲✕🍽), on the **Bidasoa River**. Follow signs towards LEITZA through more attractive villages, **Elgorriaga** (▲) and **Ituren**. Just after the latter is the tiny hamlet of **Aurtitz** (116km), directly below the sheer south face of **Mt Mendaur** (you can spot its summit chapel from the road). Walk 10 begins at Aurtitz. (*Detour:* A 5km-long, somewhat-potholed track leads from here to the Embalse de Mendaur (☂P), a beautiful shady picnic site beside Mendaur's small reservoir. You could also start Walk 10 at the reservoir, reducing the time to only 2h.)

The main tour continues ahead, passing a restored watermill, and turning left into **Zubieta** (118km), the most traditional and

20

perhaps best preserved village of the area, with its wonderful collection of houses around the square. The fascinating *zanpan-zar* procession takes place between here and Ituren on the last Monday and Tuesday in January, when locals from both villages don sheepskins and carry huge cowbells on their backs.

From here continue climbing, go through the hilltop village of **Ezkurra** (128km), and then turn right (134km) towards GOIZUETA, following the winding course of the **Urumea River**. Beyond **Goizueta** (149km ▲▲✕) there are several shady spots beside the river for a picnic, but it is best to continue on to the hamlet of **Ugaldetxo** (165km), where there are tables and other facilities to the left of the bridge beside the river (☂P).

Reaching the industrial area before Hernani (🍽), turn right on the GI132 to **Astigarraga** (174km ▲▲✕), the centre of Basque cider production. Look for the 'blue barrel' signs with the name *sagardotegia* (cider house); there are many around the town, and they serve food during the January-April season —recommended for a raucous and traditional Basque experience.

On reaching the suburb of **Loiola**, take the left fork to enter **Donostia-San Sebastián**, turning right at the Anoeta football stadium to return to our starting point (182km).

Car tour 3: The RUGGED COAST AND MOUNTAINS OF CENTRAL BIZKAIA

Bilbao • Durango • Bolibar • Lekeitio • Elantxobe • Gernika • Urdaibai Estuary • Bermeo • San Juan de Gaztelugatxe Island • Armintza • Castillo de Butrón • Bilbao

213km/132mi; about 5h driving time
En route: Short walks 4, 5, 6; Walks 11, 12, 13
Picnic suggestions: Urkiola, where Walk 12 begins (a 13km detour from Durango, the 28km-point in the tour); **Karraspio** Beach, Lekeitio (82km); near the entrance to the **Santimamiñe Caves** (a 2km detour from Kortezubi at 122km); **San Juan de Gaztelugatxe,** on the clifftops and on the island itself (149-150km); grounds of the **Castillo de Butrón** (188km)

This tour covers most of the extremely beautiful Bizkaia coastline, passing through the best-known fishing villages and exploring the dramatic seascapes of the island monastery of San Juan de Gaztelugatxe and the cliffs of Ogoño and Ermua. Other highlights include the Urdaibai Estuary Biosphere Reserve and the ancestral home of Simón Bolivar. Don't miss the short detour to the Santimamiñe Cave, with its well-preserved prehistoric paintings, and the 'painted' forest of Oma, both explored on Walk 13.

Bilbao★ (🛏🍴🛒M), the starting point for Walk 11, is the Basque Country's largest city. Among the 'sights' are the Guggenheim Museum, the bustling 'seven streets' of the old town, and many examples of award-winning modern architecture.
Leave the city from Plaza Moyua: follow signs to PLAZA ZABALBURU and TODAS DIRECCIONES, driving just to the right of the Hotel Carlton and then onto the **motorway** (2km) in the direction of DONOSTIA-SAN SEBASTIAN. Exit at JUNCTION 17 for **Durango** (28km 🛏🍴🛒)*, then take the first right turn beyond the motorway toll gate onto the N634 back towards Bilbao. Take the next right turn (30km) onto the BI3332 and then fork right again (35km) towards MUNITIBAR. At the village of **Urrutxua** (41km) continue in the

direction of MUNITIBAR. The **Bizkaiko Begiratokia/Balcón de Bizkaia** (44km 📷) is a fine viewpoint at the highest point on the road, above the forest. From here your views stretch over the green rolling hills of inland Bizkaia and to the distant Urdaibai Estuary. Continue to **Munitibar** (48km

Bridge at Ondarroa

Detour: Durango is the main base for exploring the mountains of the Duranguesado Massif, visible to the right of the motorway. To get to Walk 12, see notes on page 89.

Colegiata de Zenarruza, with the beautifully paved old pilgrims' route

⛪🏔), with its Andra Mari church, then turn right in the direction of MARKINA on the BI2224. This winding road descends through the forest to the pretty village of **Bolibar** (54km ⛪✕M), the ancestral home of the South American liberator, Simón Bolivar. The small Casa-Museo Simón Bolivar, housed in the building originally owned by the family, traces the history of his exploits (open Tue-Fri 10.00-13.00; Sat/Sun 12.00-14.00; also from 17.00-19.00 Tue-Sun in July/August).

I highly recommend the short walk from the village (35min return) up to the **Colegiata de Zenarruza**, a 15th-century former collegiate church and the only medieval abbey in Bizkaia. Start from the lane beside the Errota Taberna bar and follow the old paving of a coastal branch of the Pilgrims' Route to Santiago up through the forest (photographs above). The cloisters beside the main church are particularly attractive, and a couple of the original stations of the cross which lined the trail ascending from the village are still standing.

Leaving Bolibar, continue down the hill to the next crossroads at **Iruzubiltza** (56km), then turn left on the BI633 to **Markina-Xemein** (✕🍴) and drive on to **Ondarroa** (69km 🏔△✕🍴). Follow

'ERDIALDEA' signs, to cross the river bridge and enter the old town via the one-way system past the colourful port, one of the most active on the Bizkaia coast, and onto the BI3438 LEKEITIO road. This narrow roads meanders high above the sea through eucalyptus plantations, providing us with our first real taste of the dramatic coastline.

Just before Lekeitio, a sign to the right points to **Karraspio Beach** (82km), the best of several in the area, at the end of which are a couple of small bars and a lovely little picnic site (🛆P). Cross the river bridge to enter **Lekeitio** (83km ❄⛪🏔🏔△✕P), probably the most beautiful fishing town on the entire coast — the harbour lined with bars and restaurants, the waterfront Gothic church of Santa María de la Asunción and bay dominated by the island of San Nicolás (which may be accessed at low tide and where goats still roam).

Follow signs towards GERNIKA from the town centre on the BI638 and turn right (87km) towards ISPISTER and EA. Go right again through the small hilltop village of **Bedarona** (92km ✕), and then right on the main road through **Ea** (94km 🏔✕), with its attractive old riverside houses and stone footbridge. At the next

22

Urdaibai Estuary (Short walk 5)

Short walks for motorists
🚗 4 Ogoño

3km/1.8mi; 1h20min. Ogoño is the highest point on the vertical cliff face which rises directly above Laga Beach. It provides magnificent views both west along the Bizkaia coast and back towards Elantxobe. The route is well signposted and waymarked in yellow and is easy, apart from an initially steep ascent of 140m. Park just before the entrance to Elantxobe.

From the village square in **Elant-xobe**, with its curious turntable for buses, head left up the steep cobbled **Kale Nagusia**. Emerging by the **cemetery** (**10min**), turn right along the lane signposted to OGOÑO until you reach the last houses, from where there are great views back down to Elantxobe (**15min**).

Fork left along the track into a small wood and pass a secluded picnic spot. On reaching a gravel road (**20min**), turn right almost immediately, to re-enter the forest along a pretty path. Ignore a couple of signposted paths to the right, then climb over limestone rocks — to a clearing from where there are fantastic views down to Laga Beach directly below (**35min**). Now continue following the yellow marking over the rocks to the highest point (**40min**), with fine panoramic views.

Return the same way to **Elant-xobe** (**1h20min**).

🚗 5 San Pedro de Atxarre

3.5km/2.2 mi; 1h15min. San Pedro de Atxarre is a small hilltop chapel surrounded by holm oak forest and provides the best vantage point for views over the Urdaibai Estuary (declared a World Heritage Site and Biosphere Reserve by UNESCO in 1984). This fairly short walk involves a gradual ascent of under 100m from Akorda up through the forest. It is only signposted in a couple of places, and there is no waymarking. Park in Akorda's square, just before the Bar/Restaurante Akorda.

From the village square in **Akorda** walk a short way back along the road, to a large white **cross**. Now follow the track to the right; it enters a field for a few metres, then climbs straight ahead as a narrow path. You rise through a higher field, to a white house at the far end (**5min**), where a signpost directs you to the right along a path. Gradually climbing through holm oaks, turn right on a second path (**20min**) which levels out. At the next junction (**25min**), go straight on towards ATXERRA — a further gradual climb, on a rockier path, to the chapel of **San Pedro de Atxarre** (**40min**).

Enjoy the awesome views down to the Urdaibai Estuary and east towards the sheer cliff face of Ogoño. Then return the same way to **Akorda** (**1h15min**).

junction (97km), follow signs via **Ibarrangelua** (🏠✕) to the next fishing village, **Elantxobe** (100km ✳✕🚗🚙4). Ignore signs here to 'PORTUA'; instead, fork left and park just before the entrance to the village. From here there is a great view down to the port itself, which may be reached by walking down the incredibly steep main street from the square (driving is *not* recommended!).

Return to Ibarrangelua and turn right just beyond the village towards LAGA BEACH. (**Detour:** At 104km a turn-off to the left on the BI4236 leads to the small village of Akorda (✕🚙5) and the short walk on the previous page; allow 2.5km for this detour.)

From the junction on the main road, continue on to **Playa de Laga** (106km ✳), the beautiful stretch of sand directly below Ogoño. Follow the road hugging the coast around to the mouth of the **Urdaibai Estuary** and the second, much larger **Playa de Laida**, set back from the sea on the estuary itself. Passing the large campsite of **Kanala** (110km △), continue on the main BI635 towards GERNIKA. From **Kortezubi** (122km 🏠✕) a detour leads to the start of Walk 13 to the Santimamiñe Cave and the painted forest of Oma.

Enter **Gernika** (125km 🏨✕🚉M), made famous by the nightmare portrayed in Picasso's famous painting. Of interest here are the Casa de las Juntas, the Arbol de Gernika (the tree considered the emblem of Basque nationalism) and the attractive Parque de Europa, with several works by renowned sculptors such as Henry Moore. Following signs to BERMEO, drive along the left bank of the Urdaibai to **Mundaka** (137km ✳🏨△✕🚉), a haven for surfers, with a pretty waterfront *atalaya* affording fine views out to sea and the estuary. Continue through the large fishing port of **Bermeo** (🏨🏠✕🚉) and turn right towards BAKIO on the BI3101. The road climbs high above the sea, past a pleasant clifftop **picnic site** (149km 🚉P). Just 1km further on, at a signpost for GAZTELUGETXEKO DONIENE, turn right. This narrow lane descends steeply for 1km, to to an old stone causeway. 221 steps lead up to the chapel of **San Juan de Gaztelugatxe** (✳✝🚉P), perched atop a tiny island. The chapel, much venerated by fishermen, has been rebuilt several times over the centuries and is the site of two major pilgrimages (24th and 26th June). It is open Tue-Fri 12.00-18.00 and Sat/Sun 12.00-14.00. There is another lovely, partially covered picnic site beside the chapel.

Stone causeway and the island chapel of San Juan de Gaztelugatxe

Short walk for motorists

🚗 6 Ermua sea cliffs

4.7km/2.9 mi. 1h40min. This circuit provides an interesting contrast between the green hillsides above the bay of Gorliz, easily accessible from Bilbao, and the fascinating cliff formations below Ermua, the highest point on this part of the Bizkaia coast. Waymarking is a little haphazard, and the ascent from Fanos is quite steep until Fanos. The total ascent is 260m. On entering Gorliz, head straight down the hill past the church, following signs to 'playa/hondartza', and turn right at the seafront. Turn right up Kukulu Bidea towards the end of Astondo Beach, and park by the lane signposted 'Faro de Gorliz' (a 2km detour).

Walk up the main road (**Kukulu Bidea**) alongside a fenced-off pine forest, then turn left up a steep narrow lane called **Txosnarako Estrata** (**5min**). On reaching a gravel road, head straight across, onto a path which soon joins a lane. Veer left and continue to the end of this lane, by a farmhouse (**15min**). Now follow the track through a holm oak grove, until it becomes asphalted again, by a signpost indicating ARMINTZA/ERMUA. Carry straight on and turn left on reaching another lane (**25min**), which ends at the large **Fanos *baserri*** (**30min**).

Go through a gate and head diagonally up the hillside, enjoying your first open views of the bay of Gorliz and the green, rolling hills which descend to the sea. Turn sharp right on reaching another signpost to ERMUA (**35min**), and follow the clifftop ridge up through another holm oak grove to the summit of **Ermua** (290m; **50min**). From here you have fantastic views of the coast and to the (allegedly) dragon-shaped islet known as **Isla de Villano**.

The coastal path continues on to Armintza, but we retrace our steps back down the ridge to the signpost first passed at the 35min-point. Instead of turning left to return by the same route, go straight on. Walk through a gate and descend a clear path to the **lighthouse** (**1h15min**).

Return on the road, which initially follows the clifftops and then heads inland, to arrive back at your starting point (**1h40min**).

Continuing on the main road, just beyond the small seaside resort of **Bakio** (157km 🏖 ✕ 🅿), turn right on the BI3151, still hugging the coast. The pretty village of **Armintza** (173km ⚓✕) is dominated by its chapel on a rock jutting out to sea. From here turn right again, on to your last port of call on the Bizkaia coast, **Gorliz** (178km 🏖 △✕🅿🚗6).

From Gorliz, turn left just beyond the church, on the B2120 towards MUNGIA. Then turn right (185km) towards GATIKA and right again on the BI634 to the **Castillo de Butrón/Butroiko Gaztelua** (188km ▮✕). Another, sharp turn to the right descends to a parking area with a couple of bars. Cross the footbridge to enter the grounds of this impressive 13th-century castle, albeit much restored (open daily; in summer from 10.30-20.00; in winter from 11.00-18.30). The grounds themselves, beside the river, are very pleasant to stroll around and make a nice place to picnic (*P*).

Continuing on the main road, turn left to **Laukiz** (190km) and then right on the main BI3709 road towards BILBAO. Turn left towards DERIO (201km) and follow signs to Bilbao past the airport turn-off. Join the **motorway** (204km) and follow the blue motorway signs to pass through the **tunnel** (toll) and descend to **Bilbao**, crossing the bridge beside the Guggenheim Museum to return to Plaza Moyua (213km).

Car tour 4: BILBAO TO VITORIA-GASTEIZ VIA THE MOUNTAINS AND WATERFALLS OF SOUTHERN BIZKAIA AND WESTERN ARABA

Bilbao • (Baltzola Caves) • Artea • Itxina • Orozko • Gujuli • Orduña • (Salto del Nervión) • Puerto de Orduña • Parque Natural de Valderejo • Salinas de Añana • Mendoza • Vitoria-Gasteiz

153km/95mi; about 3h30min driving time
En route: Short walks 7, 8, 9; Walks 14, 15, 16, 17
Picnic suggestions: San Lorenzo chapel, near the **Baltzola Caves** (an 8km detour from Igorre, the 23km-point); **Pagomakurre** (at the start of Walk 14, a 9km detour from Artea at the 27km-point);

Bikatz Gene viewpoint (32km); **Delika** (81km); **Monte Santiago**, a 3km detour from the Orduña Pass at the 94km-point; **Lalastra,** the main village in the Valderejo Nature Reserve, a 17km detour from the junction with the A2622 at the 108km-point); **Villados**, beside the medieval bridge (137km)

This tour is an interesting and scenic route between Bilbao and Vitoria-Gasteiz on mainly minor roads through delightful countryside. Highlights include the landscapes of the Gorbeia and Valderejo *parques naturales* and the spectacular Sierra Salbada escarpment around the Orduña area — this is the Cantabrian-Mediterranean watershed, with the two highest waterfalls in the Basque Country. The tour is also designed to link up with Car tour 5 to Iruña-Pamplona.

From Plaza Moyua in central **Bilbao** (see Car tour 3 for further details of the city), follow signs to PLAZA ZABALBURU and TODAS DIRECCIONES, driving just to the right of Hotel Carlton and then onto the **motorway** (2km) in the direction of DONOSTIA-SAN SEBASTIAN. Exit at JUNCTION 19 onto the N240 towards VITORIA-GASTEIZ (12km). (*Detour:* From the industrial town of **Igorre** (23km 🚗), you can take an 8km detour via Dima (🏛✕) to visit the Baltzola Caves; 🚐7.) The main tour continues ahead on the N240, then forks right for **Artea** (27km 🏛✕M), where there is an interesting ethnographic museum housed in and around a beautiful old farmhouse *(Euskal Baserri)*, as well as the Museo del Nacionalismo tracing the history of Basque Nationalism. Both of these museums are only open in the summer months. A detour leads

from Artea to the start of Walk 14.
The main tour turns right at the main crossroads in Artea, on the B3513 towards OROZKO. Then take the next left turn, on a road which climbs steadily to the **Bikatz Gene** (32km 🚗🅿) viewpoint and small picnic site, affording excellent views over the valleys to the north. We now skirt the edge of the **Gorbeia Nature Reserve** and the vertical limestone wall of **Itxina** (Walk 14) comes into view ahead. Turn left into the hamlet of **Urigoiti** (37km 🏛), nestling on a hillside directly below the highest part of the rockface. There is another traditional *baserri* here — indeed, this part of Bizkaia is one of the best in the Basque Country for traditional rural architecture.
Return to the B3513 and carry on to **Orozko** (42km 🏔🏛✕), a small town with an attractive cobbled main street and old

San Lorenzo Chapel

houses overlooking the river. Crossing over the river bridge, turn left towards VITORIA-GASTEIZ, to head up the **Altube Valley**. Ignore the motorway entrance (54km); instead continue on to the **Altube Pass** (638m; 60km) and turn right (62km) towards ORDUÑA. At **Goiuri/Gujuli** (69km ✳️🏔️), turn right by the *nekazalturismoa* sign to enter this tiny village and on reaching the church, follow the sign indicating CASCADA. Park on the right just before the railway bridge and walk through a stile and over the railway line *(careful! there is no level crossing here!)*, then over another stile. From this point you get a good view of the Basque Country's highest **waterfall**, although it often has no more than a trickle of water in the summer months. Whether the river is dry or not, the view down to the valley far below is awesome, and a path may be followed for some way beside the fence. Watch your step, however, as it is very narrow and at times stays a bit too close to the edge for comfort.

Proceeding a little further along the road towards Orduña gives us our first views of the **Sierra Salbada**, the escarpment forming the Cantabrian-Mediterranean watershed — views which are increasingly spectacular as we descend to the valley bottom and re-enter Bizkaia.

Turn left to enter the village of **Artomaña** (78km) and, from the square, head beyond the village along an unmarked lane (initially on a gravel surface) to **Delika** (✖️). Turn left before the church, to pass under the railway bridge and park by a small bar/restaurant at the end of the lane, beside the river (81km 🍴P🚗8); the grassy area beside the river just beyond the bar makes a nice place to picnic.

Return through the village of

Short walk for motorists
🚗 7 Baltzola Caves

2.8km/1.7mi; 1h. This easy walk leads to caves steeped in Basque mythology. Both are entered from an extraordinary natural hollow through which a stream flows. On the return you follow the stream right through the smaller cave from one end to the other. A torch is recommended to explore the larger cave. From Igorre turn left on the BI3542 to Dima. In the town centre, turn left to Baltzola, an idyllic village with some traditional baserri. Park at the end of the road beyond the village, beside the chapel of San Lorenzo (with a small picnic site; 8 km from Igorre).

From the chapel of **San Lorenzo** (🍴P) descend the signposted lane opposite towards BALTZOLAKO KOBA. On reaching a couple of *baserri* (**5min**), continue on the track down through the forest and across the stream (**10min**), until the stream opens out into a small valley. The entrance to the smaller cave is now visible, but keep straight along the path to a **hollow** (**15min**), from where both of the **Baltzola Caves** are accessed. Circling the hollow, descend to the entrance of the larger cave, on the left (**20min**). You can walk straight through this, although towards the end things get a bit slippery. Return to the **hollow** (**35min**) and follow the path through waist-high ferns to the entrance to the smaller cave. Walk through this, following the stream back to the valley on the far side (**45min**). Cross the stream and return the same way to the chapel of **San Lorenzo** (**1h**).

Delika, past the church and the Uzkiano bar/restaurant (with economical set-price *menus*). You reach the main road and enter **Orduña** (84km 🏨♠✕; 🚌 in Amurrio 8km to the north). Orduña has an attractive main square dominated by the old *aduana* (former customs house); this is one of the very few places in the Basque Country where storks nest on the rooftops. A detour from here leads to the start of Walk 15.

Follow *SALIDA CIUDAD/HIRI IRTEERA* from the town centre to

Source of the Nervión from the Salto de Nervión (recommended detour at 94km); this photograph was taken in high summer, when the falls is only a trickle.

return to the main road towards BURGOS. This road snakes up to the top of the escarpment, briefly leaving Euskadi and entering the province of Burgos just before the **Puerto de Orduña** (900m; 93km ▢). (*Detour:* 1km beyond the pass — just before a large white obelisk — a gravel road to the left (94km) leads in 3km to the large picnic area of Monte Santiago (▢P). From there a track sign-posted SALTO DEL NERVION runs 1.8km to a platform beside the Nervión Waterfall (▢) — a fantastic viewpoint hanging out over the edge of the escarpment, more than 300m above the valley and visible from the short walk described at the right. This may be a better option at times of heavy rain than doing the walk.)

The main tour continues through **Berberena** (98km ▢); we re-enter Araba (on a noticeably better road surface!) and reach the turn-off (108km) for the **Parque Natural de Valderejo/Valderejo Parke Naturala** (Walk 16). Follow this road for 1km to **Villañane** (▢) and the **Torre-Palacio de los Varonas** (▮), the best-preserved fortified building in the province, which has been continuously inhabited for 500 years by the Varona family (open Sat/Sun/public holidays 11.00-14.00; 16.00-19.00; guided tours). Return to the A2625 towards BURGOS and, just beyond **Espejo** (▮), turn left to the **Salinas de Añana** (116km ✕▢▢9). This is the only place in the Basque Country where there are extensive salt marshes; salt extraction was the major source of employment in the area until sea salt extraction became a cheaper option by the early 20th century. The split-level terraces make a unique landscape for a short walk.

Continue towards VITORIA, turning right just after a petrol station (126km ▢) and then left through

Short walk for motorists

⚐ **8 Desfiladero del Nervión**
6.5km/4mi; 2h15min. This is a fairly level walk (total height gain 100m) which follows the course of the Nervión upstream to the immense cliff face of the escarpment (shown opposite), close to its source. After periods of heavy rain, especially in winter, a waterfall plunges over 300m at the start of the river's journey to the Bilbao estuary. Note that the last part of the walk crosses the river several times, which may make the going more tricky in winter, although when the river bed is dry it is possible to get practically to the base of the escarpment. Regardless of the time of year, this is an extremely beautiful walk.

From the bar/restaurant at **Delika**, go through the gate and follow the narrow path to the right of the stream, crossing a stile (**5min**) and continuing along a farm track to an old **stone bridge** (**10min**). Take the left-hand track here (a fence to the right encircles some woodland on the far side of the stream). The track ascends gradually and then levels out (**20min**) as the escarpment comes into view directly ahead. Go right at the next fork (**25min**) and right again at the following one (**40min**). Pass an animal trough and reach the river and the **end of the track** (**45min**). From this point follow a path close to the river, going over a stile and crossing the river several times as you enter a narrow gorge, the **Desfiladero del Nervión**. A viewing platform at the Salto del Nervión (a detour from the Orduña Pass) is visible at the top of the escarpment to the right as you turn the final bend towards the base of the cliff and the waterfall. (The

Continues overleaf

path ends here (**1h10min**), and of course the amount of water in the falls depends on the time of year.

Retrace your steps to where you last crossed the river; re-cross it (**1h35min**) and, at the first junction after the path widens, take the left-hand fork to cross the river again (**1h40min**). Then follow the track downstream on the opposite bank through gall oak and beech forest. This track maintains a reasonable height above the river, but descends to cross it one more time (**2h05min**), to return to the old stone bridge and **Deika** (**2h15min**).

Short walk for motorists

🚗 9 Salinas de Añana

2km/1.2mi; 40min. A short but interesting circuit around the terraces used for salt collection, now being restored after years of neglect. Park by the church on the main road in Salinas de Añana.

Walk up the main road through **Salinas de Añana** and turn right to the **Convento de San Juán de Acre** (**15min**). Follow the path beside the convent wall to a *mirador* (**20min**), the best viewpoint over the terraces. Take the next right-hand fork, down to the head of the valley, and return on the far side. Cross the stream at the lower end (taste the salt in it!) and return to **Salinas de Añana** (**40min**).

Orduña: church in the main square

Nanclares de Oca (133km). (***Detours:*** Beyond this town, short detours to the left of 1km and 3km respectively lead to the beautiful medieval bridges of Villados (137km 🚏*P*) and Trespuentes crossing the river Zadorra.) Turn left to **Mendoza** (**M**), dominated by a fortified tower which now houses the Heraldry Museum of Araba, a fascinating exhibition of family coats of arms from the region (open 1 May-11 Oct: Tue-Fri 11.00-14.00 and 16.00-20.00; Sat 11.00-15.00, Sun 10.00-14.00). From here a pretty road winds through this fertile countryside, with fine views of hilltop villages, to the outskirts of **Vitoria-Gasteiz** (151km). From the roundabout by the petrol station (🚏), head straight on, following signs to CENTRO/ERDIALDEA. Cross over the dual carriageway, to the Cathedral of Santa María, and from there head on to the CASCO MEDIEVAL (old quarter) and the CORREO (post office) in the city centre (153km).

Bales of hay just south of Puerto de Orduña

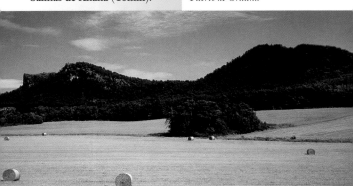

Car tour 5: The WINE-GROWING AREA OF RIOJA ALAVESA, THE MONTAÑA ALAVESA, AND THE SIERRAS OF TOLOÑO-CANTABRIA, URBASA AND ARALAR

Vitoria-Gasteiz • Faido • Peñacerrada • Laguardia • Kripan • La Población • Kanpezu • Contrasta • Sierra de Urbasa • San Miguel de Aralar • Sierra de Aralar • Lekunberri • Iruña-Pamplona

211km/131mi; about 5h driving time
En route: Short walks 10, 11, 12; Walks 17, 18, 19, 20, 21, 22
Picnic suggestions: Balcón de Rioja (39km); **source of the Kripan River** (a 2km detour from

Kripan at the 63km-point); **Santuario de Kodes** (an 11km detour from the 74km-point, not far past La Población); **Sierra de Urbasa** (122km); **San Miguel de Aralar** (166km); **Albia** (170km)

T his tour can be enjoyed in its own right or can be combined with Car tour 4. It is a linear route from Vitoria-Gasteiz to Iruña-Pamplona along scenic minor roads. It covers the little-known Montaña Alavesa, the wine-growing area of Rioja Alavesa and the Sierras of Toloño-Cantabria, Urbasa and Aralar, all with their unique landscapes. Much of the terrain lies in areas protected by three different nature reserves, so there are plenty of opportunities to get out of the car and do some fine walking.

Vitoria-Gasteiz (✝♨⚠✕⌘M) has more green spaces per inhabitant than any other city in Spain. Also notable are the recently-restored Gothic Cathedral of Santa María, the Fournier Museum of Playing Cards, the beautiful *casco medieval* (old quarter) and many cycle tracks leading from the city centre right out into the countryside (free bicycle hire from the tourist office, with collection points around the city). Walk 17 is easily reached from the centre.
Starting in the centre by the **post office** *(correo)* drive along **Calle Olagüibel** and turn right into **Calle de la Paz**, past the Corte Inglés department store. From here follow signs to PEÑACERRADA and LOGROÑO , crossing the railway line and leaving the built-up area (2km). At the **round-about** just on the edge of the city, turn left and then take the first right turn, on the A2124 to PEÑACERRADA, crossing the **Puerto de Vitoria** (758m; 9km).

Turn left (11km) to the tiny village of **San Vicentejo**, to see the interesting **Ermita de la Inmaculada**, then continue south on the A2124. At the crossroads just before the Venta de Armentia (a large bar and restaurant; ✕ 14km), turn left on the CL127 towards OBECURI, and then take the next right, following signs for CUEVAS ARTIFICIALES. You can visit these caves on a short walk from the pretty village of **Faido** (22km ♨∩⌘10).
Go back along the road out of the village and, just after a small walled cemetery, turn left up a fairly potholed road to the church in the hamlet of **Baroja**. From there rejoin the A2124 and turn left to continue to **Peñacerrada** (31km ✝♨⚠✕❄). At the entrance to the village is an 18th-century working *errota* (watermill), which still makes flour for the adjacent bakery; the rest of the building being a beautifully-restored *casa rural* (tel: 945 367005). The village itself is largely walled, with

31

Short walks for motorists

🚶 **10 Cuevas artificiales de Faido — 'little Cappadoccia'**
3.5km/2.2mi; 1h. An interesting, easy walk visiting two of the hundred or so man-made caves that were first lived in by hermits in this part of Araba and the Condado de Treviño (Burgos province) as early as the 6th century, and in particular the 13th-century cave chapel of Nuestra Señora de la Peña.

In **Faido** an information board with map details the route and history of the caves. The seven permanent residents take it in turns as custodians of the chapel; anyone will tell you who has the key. Follow signs to the CASA RURAL and then along a track, forking left up the path to the **cave chapel**. Climb up on the rocks above it, to visit a second small **cave** beside the belfry (**15min**). Return to the track and follow it round to the other side of the field, where a fairly overgrown path through the woods leads to the **caves of San Miguel**, the larger one of which contains a small **shrine** (**35min**).
Retrace your steps to **Faido** (**1h**).

🚶 **11 La Población**
3.6km/2.2mi; 1h15min. A short and safe walk, but with a steep climb of 300m to the pointed peak of La Población (photograph overleaf), an incredible viewpoint over Rioja and neighbouring mountains.

At **La Población** follow the track which starts just past the **church** and veers right behind some houses (ignore the SL.NA195 in front of the houses). Turn sharp left (**10min**) to join the start of the summit path; this zigzags up to a fine viewpoint towards the long Sierra Tolona-Cantabria to the west and Ioar to the east (**30min**). Continue to the top of **La Población** (**40min**).
Return the same way to the village **church** (**1h15min**).

the gateway at the southern end being particularly impressive.
Keeping to the A2124, the next point of interest along the route is the **Balcón de Rioja/Errioxako Ikkuspegia** (39km 🚗🅿P), an extraordinary viewpoint (with picnic site) over the plains of Rioja at the point where the road cuts through the Sierra de Toloño-Cantabria.
Descend to the plain to enter Rioja Alavesa, the northern part of the wine-growing area still within the *Comunidad Autónoma Vasca*. Turn left along the A124 to reach the beautiful walled town of **Laguardia★** (50km 🚻🏨🛏🍴🅿), backed by the jagged peaks of the Sierra de Toloño-Cantabria. Visit the *centro histórico*, whose focal point is the church of Santa María de los Reyes with its extraordinarily ornate portico (key from the local tourist office on the main road). The tourist office can also organise a visit to one of the many wine *bodegas* in the area.
From Laguardia take the A3228 towards ELVILLAR but, just before the village, turn left to **la Chabola de la Hechicera** (55km 🪨), one of the best-preserved dolmens in the Basque Country. From **Elvillar** continue straight on to **Kripan** (63km). (*Detour:* Just before Kripan, by the km 74 marker, a partially-asphalted lane to the left leads in 2km to a shady picnic site (🅿P) by the source (*nacedero*) by the Kripan River. Walk 18 can start here, or from the village of Kripan itself.)
Just beyond Kripan, follow signs towards BERNEDO on the A3220 and turn right to enter the hilltop village of **La Población** (69km 🚗🚶11), from where you can take an unforgettable walk to the top of the mountain of the same name. (Or, if you prefer, just walk *round* the mountain on the new SL.NA195 signposted footpath.)
Carry on through the village along

Contrasta (top) and gateway at the southern end of Peñacerrada (right)

a scenic hilltop road past a large wind farm, and turn left on the NA7211 (74km) towards GENE-VILLA. (A right turn at this point leads to Aguilar and the start of Walk 19; ⊞*P*.) The road cuts back through a gap in the sierra to re-enter the Montaña Alavesa. At the main crossroads in **Kanpezu** (82km ✖🍽), turn right towards ESTELLA. (A left turn here leads towards Vitoria-Gasteiz and Antoñana, and the start of Walk 20.)

Follow CENTRO URBANO signs to enter Kanpezu's old town. From here take the A2128 road towards CONTRASTA; this winds through the rolling farmland of the Arana Valley via some idyllic villages, most notably **San Vicente de Arana** (92km ✖; the only village in the valley with a place to eat). Go through the pretty walled village of **Contrasta** (97km 🏰) and take the next right turn. Beyond **Larraona**, turn left on the NA718 (113km) towards OLAZTI. (A right turn leads to Zudaire (🏨✖🍽), Estella, and Walk 21.)

We now enter the Sierra de Urbasa as we approach the immense cliff face of the **Balcón de Pilatos**; stop at the viewpoint (117km 📷) and, just after entering the **Parque Natural de Urbasa** (✳), park on a gravel area marked *aparcadero* (119km). From here the top of the cliff face can be reached on foot: walk straight ahead from the end of the car park for five minutes, then follow the fence for 10 minutes, around to the projecting rock visible from the head of the Urederra Valley (see Walk 21). During the Spanish Civil War, Franco's troops allegedly pushed Republican prisoners off this rock in order to save bullets.

From here the road crosses the plateau of the **Sierra de Urbasa**, where there are many fine picnic spots, the best being to the right, close to a small shepherd's hut which has been converted into an information centre and where there is an interesting restored *txondorra* (charcoal kiln; 122km ⊞*P*). Urbasa sheep's cheese is

Above: La Población from the north, near Kanpezu. The eponymous village is on the south side of the mountain.

famous, so look out for several places along the way selling *ardi gazta*. Just after the **main park office** (129km), where maps may be obtained detailing several walks in the Sierra, the road descends dramatically through a gap in the rocks to **Olazti** (136km) on the **Plain of Araba**.

Turn right on the main road and follow the N240 signs towards IRUÑA-PAMPLONA. Soon after passing the long ridge of **San Donato** to the right, turn off at JUNCTION 34 for UHARTE-ARAKIL (154km), and follow the purple sign towards ARALARKO SAN MIGUEL/SAN MIGUEL DE ARALAR, the sanctuary visible high up on the mountain ahead.

Take the first left turn on the NA2410, around the back of **Uharte-Arakil**, passing an old stone bridge to the right, then take

the narrow road signposted to SAN MIGUEL DE ARALAR (156km). The road rises steeply through beautiful forest. On reaching the top of the ridge, turn right to park beside **San Miguel de Aralar** (166km (✳♦ 🖼)), with its Romanesque church. The views from here are awesome — especially across the valley towards the long ridge of San Donato. It is possible to eat your own food at the tables inside the *hospedaría* beside the church; otherwise, simple meals and drinks are served, and the hilltop area around the sanctuary makes an excellent **picnic site** (🪑P).

From the sanctuary continue down the hill to the **Guardetxe/ Casa Forestal de Aralar** (169km ✳✕🛈), the main base for walks in the **Sierra de Aralar** and the starting point for Walk 22. The road continues through karst rock formations and dense forest in the heart of the sierra, making for a delightful drive. The parking area for **Albia** (170km 🛈P) is another

good base from which to explore or picnic.
(***Detour:*** At 181km, just before Lekunberri, a detour of 3km to the right leads to the tiny village of Iribas (🚗12).)
The main tour continues straight on to the crossroads at **Lekunberri** (182km ⛰△✕⛽), where you turn right on the NA130, to join the A15 dual carriageway to IRUÑA-PAMPLONA at JUNCTION 123. The road passes through a gorge flanked by one of Nafarroa's best-known natural landmarks — **Biaizpe/Dos Hermanas**, rocks known as the 'Two Sisters' (192km), then enters the flat, fertile plain of the Pamplona basin at **Irurtzun**. Leave the motorway at JUNCTION 88 (206km), to enter **Iruña-Pamplona**. Follow the long Avenida de Pio XII towards ZONA CENTRO, and turn right just after the main park. You pass the old ramparts and reach Plaza de La Paz by the bus station (211km).

Short walk for motorists

(🚗 12 Nacederos de Iribas)

5km/3.1mi; 1h30min. This route explores the curious geological phenomenon of the two sources of the Ertzilla River — the first source emerging from the cliff face of Aitzarrateta, the second source being where the river re-emerges after its underground journey, just below the village of Iribas. The walk is waymarked throughout in green and white. Overall ascent of under 100m. Park just before the entrance to the village, beside a map providing details of the route.

Walk through the village of **Iribas** following the green and white waymarking, past the *frontón* and onto an unsurfaced road (**5min**). This ascends gradually. At the first fork (**15min**), head right and, at the second (**20min**), go left, to descend along a path past a *borda* and down to the river (**30min**). Turn right to follow the crystal-clear **Ertzilla River** beside moss-covered rocks and thick vegetation — a magical place! You pass the remains of an **old mill** and reach the cliff face of **Aitzarrateta** (**35min**), from where the **river emerges for the first time**.

Retrace your steps along the river, but this time keep straight on beside it, still in the forest, until you reach the point where the river carves a U-shape and then disappears underground (**55min**). The path crosses to the other side and contines as a farm track. You reach a circular walled area, within which is the huge **Lezegalde Chasm** (**1h05min**). Walk round the top of the chasm and follow the path down a dry valley to the **second source of the Ertzilla** (**1h20min**).

From here a path climbs steeply up above the left bank of the river, back to **Iribas** (**1h30min**).

Car tour 6: THE PYRENEAN VALLEYS AND HISTORIC TOWNS OF NORTH/CENTRAL NAFARROA

Iruña-Pamplona • Olite • Sangüesa • Castillo de Javier • Lumbier • Foz de Arbaiun • Ochagavia • Orreaga/Roncesvalles • Auritz/Burguete • Iruña-Pamplona

258km/160miles; about 5h driving
En route: Short walks 13, 14, 15, 16; Walks 23, 24, 25
Picnic suggestions: Foz de Lumbier (133km); **Ochagavia** (165km) — either 1km beyond the village, **beside the river** or at the **Santuario de Muskilda** (a 4km detour, also on the route of Short walk 16); **Casas de Irati**, at the start of Walk 24 in the Forest of Irati (a 23km detour from Ochagavia); **Col d'Ibañeta** (208km); **Zandueta** (223km)

Nafarroa is by far the largest of the seven provinces covered in this book, and the most varied. This tour covers many of the most scenic corners of the more arid, central part of the province. Highlights include the *foces* (gorges), towns and villages steeped in history going back to Roman times, the verdant Pyrenean valleys of Salazar and Aezkoa, Irati (one of Europe's largest forested areas) and finally the collegiate church of Orreaga/Roncesvalles, one of the major starting points in Spain for the Pilgrims' Route to Santiago.

Iruña-Pamplona★ (✝▲△✕⛽) is famous for its week-long San Fermines festival during the second week in July, with the running of the bulls *(encierro)*. There is also an historic old town with ramparts to be seen.

From the Plaza de la Paz by the bus station in the city centre, go along **Avenida del Ejército**, then turn left, following signs to the ZONA HOSPITALARIA along **Avenida de Pio XII**. Keep straight on out of the city, joining the motorway at JUNCTION 88 in the direction of ZARAGOZA (5km). Pass the impressive 18th-century **Noain Aqueduct** (12km) and

Right: Olite; below: cutting grass near Pamplona

continue south. At 42km turn off at JUNCTION 50 for OLITE and follow the N121 into the centre of **Olite** (47km 🏨🛌⛺🍴✕🅿). Park to the left of the entrance gate to the beautifully preserved historic old town, dominated by the 14th-century former Royal Palace. Built by Carlos II, part of the palace has now been converted into a *parador* (open 10.00-14.00 and 16.00-20.00 in summer; closes slightly earlier in the afternoon the rest of the year).

Continue left around the town, onto the NA5300, and drive through vineyards to **San Martín de Unx** (57km ✕). (*Detour:* A right turn just beyond San Martín de Unx leads to the picture-postcard medieval hilltop village of Ujúe (☀🏨⛰✕☎🚌13), dominated by the large 12th/13th-century church-fortress of Santa María, overlooking terraced hillsides. The village streets form a winding maze — much too narrow and steep for cars.

The main tour continues on the N132 through vineyards, with

wind farms lining the long ridges on both sides of the road. (*Detour:* A turn-off right (72km) leads to Gallipienzo (☎), another small hilltop village above a bend in the Aragón River.)

The main tour goes straight on, crosses the Aragón, and enters the historic city of **Sangüesa/Zangoza** (87km 🏨⛺△✕🅿). The church of Santa María La Real, with its famed portico, is just to the left after the bridge (guided tours arranged by the tourist office directly opposite). Proceed along Calle Mayor, following signs for JAVIER on the NA5410. There is a well-known castle at **Javier** (95km 🏰✕), the birthplace of the patron saint of Nafarroa, San Franciso Javier.

Cross the **Irati River** (100km) and carry on to **Yesa** (⛺✕), then turn left on the main road towards IRUÑA-PAMPLONA. (*Detour:* A right turn almost immediately leads to the Monasterio de Leire (☀☎) and the start of Walk 23 to Arangoiti — the long ridge to parallel to the road.)

At the major junction of **Liedena** (107km 🅿) continue towards IRUÑA-PAMPLONA until the sheer walls of the Foz de Lumbier come into view on the right, by a convenient viewpoint (109km). Take the next right turn on the NA150, towards LUMBIER

Short walk for motorists

🚗 **13 El Camino de las Pilas**
*5.8km/3.6mi; 1h45min. This circuit
explores some of the terraced hillsides
surrounding Ujúe, passing some
abandoned farmsteads and the pilas
de agua (places for washing clothes)
used up until 1952, when piped
water reached the village. Parts of the
route are quite overgrown and there
is a fairly steep ascent from the pilas
back to the village. Overall ascent:
150m. In general the walk is well
waymarked in green and white, and
signposted SL.NA177A. Park at the
entrance to Ujúe, an 8km detour
from San Martín de Unx.*

Starting from the ruined church of
San Miguel at the bottom end of
Ujúe, where there is a board
detailing the route, follow the
track downhill, turning left almost
immediately. You descend to the
bottom of the valley and join
another track (**15min**): follow this
to the left, to pass the ruins of the
Corral de Porta. From here the
remains of an old **watermill** may
be seen by the stream, to the right
(**25min**). Cross the stream, then
take the first track to the left, to
continue beside the stream to the
remains of a second farmstead, the
Corral del Fausto (**45min**).
Vines cover the narrow valley
floor, and from here the path —
although reasonably well
waymarked — becomes very
overgrown, as you make your way
to the ruins of the old *pilas*
(**55min**).

Continue through the long grass
past the *pilas*, cross the stream
(**1h**) and follow the old *cañada
real* (drover's road) which zigzags
up the terraced hillside to the
highest point at a small pass, **El
Portillo de las Pilas** (**1h20min**).
From here Ujúe comes into view
again, and it is a simple walk back
to the road (**1h30min**). Follow
the lower road, to the left of **Ujúe**,
back down to the church of **San
Miguel** (**1h45min**).

(113km). (***Detour:*** At the crossroads just before the town centre,
turn right along a narrow lane to
the Foz de Lumbier (🚗**14**). The
lane ends after 1.5km, at a car park
a short way before the entrance to
the Foz.)

From the centre of **Lumbier**
(116km ✳△✕🚻) continue
straight on towards NAVASCUES.
On the right at the top of the **Iso
Pass** (129km ✳🚗) is the main
viewpoint over the **Foz de
Arbaiun**, an immense canyon
through which the Salazar flows.
Many birds of prey are also easily
spotted here, perching on rocks on
the higher part of the canyon, so
have the binoculars ready again.
The whole canyon is 6km long,
and the far end may be clearly seen
from the Arangoiti ridge in the
course of Walk 23.

Continuing up the valley, we pass
a turn-off left (134km). (***Detour:***
This leads towards Aspurz and
🚗**15**.) Continue to the crossroads
at the sleepy town of **Navascues**

Short walk for motorists

🚗 **14 Foz de Lumbier**

*5.8km/3.6mi; 1h45min. This is an excellently waymarked circuit (green and white, signposted SL.NA113) above and through the Foz de Lumbier, an impressive gorge through which the Irati River flows. The return route through the gorge follows the old Pamplona-Sangüesa railway line through two tunnels (a **torch** is highly recommended, although plenty of people manage without). Total height gain: 200m. Look out for the many griffon vultures and other birds of prey which nest in the gorge — binoculars essential! Park in the car park before the entrance to the gorge.*

From the **Foz de Lumbier car park** carry on along the lane beyond (closed to vehicles) to a small picnic site (**5min**; 🍴P) with a spring. Then turn left to follow the waymarked path as it climbs up to the plateau, where you join a wide track (**20min**). The chapel of

Trinidad is visible to the left on the top of the ridge.

At the point where the track levels out (**30min**), turn right and, later, turn right again, to descend to within sight of the **Irati River**, Join a path which emerges on the old railway line beside the river (**45min**). Follow this to the entrance to the **first tunnel** (**1h**). Just *before* going through this tunnel, turn left on an extremely narrow path — which is also very slippery after rain — to see the ruins of a bridge, the **Puente del Infierno**, which crosses the entrance to the gorge.

Return to the tunnel (**1h15min**) and walk through it to enter the **Foz de Lumbier** proper, passing through a **second tunnel**. At the far end you emerge by the path you ascended at the start of the walk. Retrace your steps to the **car park** (**1h45min**).

(139km), forking left to continue along the Salazar Valley via **Oronoz** (160km 🚗) to the riverside village of **Escaróz** (162km 🏠✕), with its delightful main cobbled street and square.

Fork right to enter **Ochagavía** (165km 👶🏠✕🚗16), one of Pyrenean Nafarroa's most attractive villages, at the confluence of two rivers which flow into the Salazar. The Anduña River runs through the centre of the village, flanked on both sides by the

typical old stone houses of the region. Cobbled streets lead off up towards the fortress-like church of San Juan Evangelista. This is an extremely popular touring centre, and the many *casas rurales* fill up quickly in high season and at weekends; either book in advance or be prepared to stay at other nearby villages (Escaróz, Jaurrieta, Izalzu or the villages in the neighbouring Roncal Valley all have similar accommodation). There is a nice riverside picnic site

Short walks for motorists

🚐 **15 Foz de Santa Colomba**
3.1km/2mi; 1h15min. This circuit (green and white waymarking, signposted SL.NA111) follows the course of the little-known Foz de Santa Colomba, not as spectacular as the two previous foces visited on this tour, but well off the beaten track and a very pleasant short walk. Shorts are not recommended, due to the proliferation of prickly bushes invading the path. The walk crosses the gorge itself, which may involve a bit of wading at certain times of the year; the ascent from the gorge is also quite steep. Total height gain: 120m.
Turn left over the bridge towards Aspurz and park in the car park on the left about 200m further on.

From the **car park** follow the path behind the explanatory map detailing the route, through quite thick vegetation. Take the first left-hand fork (**5min**) to walk above the **Salazar River** along a narrow stony path, then descend to the right, to an old **stone bridge** at the entrance to the **Foz de Santa Colomba** (**20min**).

Cross the bridge and follow the path through even thicker vegetation, quite close to the **Egúrzanos River** (which is practically dry in the summer months). The path ends at the point where the valley narrows to the **gorge proper** (**40min**). Look for the waymarking on the opposite bank and some handrails in the rock, and cross the gorge, which may involve a little wading outside of the driest months. Then continue up the ravine on the far side, climbing to a fine **viewpoint** (**50min**) over the scenic, uninhabited valley beyond the gorge.

From here continue climbing quite steeply, to a clearing above the forest (**1h**), from where a track descends abruptly back to the **car park** (**1h15min**).

The 12th-century Santuario de Muskilda, restored in the 17th century

🚐 **16 Santuario de Muskilda**
6.2km/3.8mi; 2h. Another SL green and white circuit (SL.NA65), also coinciding with the GR11 Trans-Pyrenean route at the start. We visit the 12th-century Romanesque chapel of Muskilda perched on top of the heavily-forested hill of the same name above Ochagavía. This is a splendid viewpoint over the valley and the forest is wonderfully shady. Total height gain: 295m. Park in the centre of Ochagavía.

From **Ochagavía** walk up the cobbled street behind the **church** until you reach the last houses in the village (**5min**). Follow the GR11 markings to the right, on an attractive cobbled trail which climbs fairly steeply up though the forest, past **stations of the cross**, to the **Santuario de Muskilda** (**35min**). Walk right, through the entrance gate and courtyard, passing a small picnic site (🚐*P*). Join the road and turn right almost immediately, to re-enter the forest on the SL.NA65. After passing a rather incongruous **water tank** at the top of the hill, descend to cross the road (**55min**) and continue along a track which emerges on the open mountain just before the **Borda Xubri** (**1h10min**).

From here the GR11 continues over the long ridge of Abodi ahead, but we turn sharp left, to begin our return route through the forest, past a **spring** to the right (**1h20min**). The path widens to a track and bends sharply down to the right (**1h35min**). At this point we carry straight on along a narrow forest path, back to the top end of **Ochagavía** (**2h**).

Short walk 15: Foz de Santa Colomba

($\bar{\mathbb{A}}P$) about 1km beyond the village towards Isaba. Walk 24 in the Irati Forest begins 23km north of Ochagavía.

Returning to **Escaróz** (168km), turn right over the bridge on the NA140 towards JAURRIETA and AURITZ/BURGUETE. This mountain road passes through **Abaurre-gaina/Abaurrea Alta** (181km), the highest village in Nafarroa at 1035m, with great views towards the Pyrenees. From here the road descends, with continually fine views of the mountains, to **Aribe** (192km 🏨 🏚), with its triple-arched medieval bridge over the Irati River. Aribe is the base for a detour to Orbaitzeta and the start of Walk 25.

Continue on the main road. (Just beyond Aribe, about 100m to the left along the road towards OROZ BETELU, is an impressive crag which may be climbed in a few minutes from the car park, and from where there are excellent views of the Irati River and Gorge.) On reaching the main N135 road, turn right to enter **Auritz/Burguete** (201km 🏨🏨 △✕🏚), one of the prettiest villages in the region, with lovely old houses and water channels lining its main street. It is worth stopping here, as there are several fine accommodation and eating possibilities.

From here a tree-lined avenue soon brings us to **Orreaga/Roncesvalles** (206km ✝✕). This important sanctuary and hospital is the most popular starting point in Spain for the Pilgrims' Route to Santiago. It is also the site of the legendary battle of Roncesvalles in 778, when the Basques defeated Charlemagne's army, as immortalised in the *Chanson de Roland*, which spread the word of Christianity. Carry on up to the **Col d'Ibañeta** (1057m; 208km 📷), where a monolith commemorates the battle and there is an interesting bird migration centre. During September and October, the centre sets up several telescopes on the col which may be used by the public for observing the thousands of migrating birds as they cross this relatively low part of the Pyrenees. The col also makes a fine picnic area ($\bar{\mathbb{A}}P$). (See *Landscapes of the Pyrenees* for details of walks in this area.) From here it is also possible to descend into France to St Jean-Pied-de-Port/Donibane Garazi and link up with Car tour 8.

Return via **Auritz/Burguete** on the main road and take the next left turn, the NA172 towards AOIZ/AGOITZ. This scenic road follows the course of the **Urrobi River**, passing several small hamlets with old stone cottages. One of them, **Zandueta** (223km $\bar{\mathbb{A}}P$), has a nice little picnic site to the left by the river. Leaving the forested area, the valley widens out to rolling farmland. We cross the **Canal de Navarra** (237km) just before Aoiz/Agoitz. Turn right at the roundabout just before this town, to gain the NA150 to IRUÑA-PAMPLONA.

On arriving at the outskirts of the city (252km), turn left on the dual carriageway, then follow the N135 and signs to CENTRO URBANO/ERDI ALDEA. Entering **Iruña-Pamplona** proper, keep straight ahead towards DONOSTIA-SAN SEBASTIAN on the N240, to return to the bus station (258km).

Car tour 7: THE FRENCH BASQUE COAST AND PICTURESQUE INLAND VILLAGES OF LAPURDI

Bayonne/Baiona • Biarritz • (Guethary) • St Jean-de-Luz/Donibane Lohizun • La Corniche • Ascain • Ainhoa • Espelette • Pas de Roland • Bidarrai • Cambo-les-Bains • Route des Cimes • Mougerre • Bayonne/Baiona

151km/94mi; about 4h30min driving time
En route: Short walks 3, 17; Walks 26, 27, 28, 29
Picnic suggestions: St Jean-de-Luz/Donibane Lohizun, on the **Sainte Barbe** headland at far of

the beach (31km); **Domaine d'Abbadie**, Hendaia (40km); **Pas de Roland**, beside the river (92km); **Baztán Gorge** (a 2km detour from Bidarrai at the 101km-point, on the way to the start of Walk 28)

This tour covers the rugged French Basque coast and its attractive resorts, combined with the beautiful villages of inland Lapurdi and undulating countryside of the Pyrenean foothills.

Bayonne/Baiona (✝♙△✕🍴M) has a Gothic cathedral, the Musée Bonat and an interesting old town (Petit Bayonne). Start the tour from the tourist office: make for the nearest roundabout, just before the river, and follow signs on the D5 towards ANGLET-PLAGES. This road keeps parallel to the **Adour River** at the start of the estuary. When you reach the mouth of the river (6km), turn right to **la Barre**, the lighthouse and breakwater at the mouth of the river — a good point from which to observe the shipping activity and sea. From the roundabout at la Barre, follow signs towards BIARRITZ; from here on, lanes lead off to the right, to a string of pleasant beaches. Leave the built-up area (10km) at a roundabout, following signs for GROTTE DE LA CHAMBRE D'AMOUR, to return to the coast and a road which initially runs below the cliffs. The road then climbs up to the top of the cliffs, close to the **Pointe St Martin lighthouse**. You are now entering the stylish resort of **Biarritz★** (♙△✕🍴) proper. On arriving in the town centre, take the first right turn at the first traffic lights (by the Hotel du Palais; 13.5km) towards PORT

VIEUX. In this way you avoid the often-congested town centre and can drive along the most spectacular stretch of coast around Biarritz. The old port itself, on the right opposite the church of Saint-Eugenie, is well worth exploring. Continuing through a tunnel under the cliff, you arrive at the **Roche de la Vierge** (15km ✲📷), the French Basque coast's best-known landmark. A walk across the footbridge to the rock topped by a statue of the Virgin Mary, provides an exhilarating short stroll, especially when the sea is high and the waves come crashing in around the rock and spew out through a natural arch jutting out from the cliffs.
Continue around the small **Plage du Port Vieux** and follow signs on D911 towards ST JEAN-DE-LUZ. Turn right on the main N10 road (21km) and proceed through **Bidart** (24km), where the road again reaches the sea by the village's main beach, and above Guethary (25km). (***Detour:*** It's worth turning right from the traffic lights at the top of the hill to divert 1km to this pretty village (♙△✕) with its tiny fishing port.)
On reaching **St Jean-de-Luz/**

Sara

Donibane Lohizun (⛰△✕⛽ ⛩**M**), follow the bypass road round the town towards DONOSTIA-SAN SEBASTIAN. Once down at the roundabout by the main **railway station** (31km), turn right to park and explore the fishing port and very attractive old town centre. Of special interest is the Maison Louis XIV, where the young king was married (on the main square of the same name) and a nice picnic site (⛩*P*) at the far end of the beach on the **Sainte Barbe** headland.

Leaving St Jean, cross the bridge over the river Nive and take first right turn, to enter **Ziburu-Ciboure** and return to the road which hugs the bay. At **Sokoa** you cross a small bridge over the river and head along the D912 towards HENDAYE-PLAGE — to the start of **La Corniche** (34km ✻📷), the beautiful cliff-top drive towards the Spanish border. Go straight over a first roundabout just before the border town of **Hendaye/ Hendaia** (⛰△✕), then turn right on a lane (40km) to the **Domaine d'Abbadie** (✻**M***P*🚗17). The

Short walk for motorists

🚗 17 Chateau d'Abbadie

4km/2.5mi; 1h40min. This leisurely stroll (but with a steep descent of 80m to the Baie de Loya) takes in some of the most dramatic cliff formations on the Basque coast in an area of fields and woodland forming part of the estate of the Chateau d'Abbadie.

From the **car park** just before the beach, enter the estate along a signposted gravel path. Just before reaching the **Larretxea information centre**, turn left and cross the field, to the start of the cliff path. Once above the cliffs, a **viewpoint** overlooks the end of the excellent sandy beach of Hendaye/Hendaia (**10min**). Now follow the cliffs and, where there is a choice of paths, take the one closest to the cliff-tops for the best views. Twin offshore rocks, **Les Deux Jumeaux** (**20min**), are home to many cormorants. According to legend, these rocks were thrown from the top of the Aiako Harriak (Peñas de Aia; Walk 7) by the angry *basojaun* (giant) guarding the mountain.

Continue around the cove here, past some large derelict WW2 **bunkers**, to **Pointe Ste Anne** (**30min**), the main headland, offering fine views to some of the best sandstone cliff formations and back to the château perched on the highest part of the estate. The coastal path circles round the cliffs and enters some woodland (**40min**). Emerging from the wood, a signposted diversion to the left (**50min**) leads down a steep path to the **Baie de Loya** (**1h05min**).

Climb back to the crossroads (**1h25min**) and continue past a farmhouse, with the château just to your left, to the information centre (**1h35min**), then return along the gravel path to the **car park** (**1h40min**).

estate, and especially the Pointe Ste Anne headland, makes a good spot for a picnic with sea views. The château was originally built in the mid-19th century by a half-Irish, half-Basque adventurer and explorer, Antoine d'Abbadie, best remembered for his research work close to the sources of the Nile in Ethiopia and his correspondence with the poet Rimbaud. Returning to the same round-about, turn left towards PARC FLORENIA, to join the N10 again (44km). Turn left again in the direction of BAYONNE.

On reaching a roundabout in **Urrugne** (49km ▲ △ ✕), turn right under the motorway bridge on the D4 towards ASCAIN and SARA/SARE. The road now heads inland towards the Pyrenean foothills as they fall away into the Atlantic. Continue on this road towards SARA, taking the left fork (52km) towards OLHETTE. When the road reaches the highest point in **Olhette** (55km), opposite a salmon-coloured *frontón*, a country lane to the right, signposted LE CHEMIN DE MONTTUBAITA, leads in 1km to a large farmhouse, a *gîte d'étape* and the start of Walk 26 to Larrun.

From Olhette the road follows the flanks of Larrun and soon reaches the pretty village of **Ascain** (61km ▲ △ ✕). At the clock tower by the main square, turn right towards SARE. The road climbs to the funicular station of **Le Petit Train de la Rhune** ★ (65km). An easy alternative to Walk 26 is to take the train up and return back down the mountain on a waymarked path which ends at the funicular station.

The road meanders downhill. At the first roundabout, head straight up the hill to the square in the centre of **Sara** (68 km ▲ △ ✕), another picture-postcard tradi-tional Basque village. A beautiful

tamarisk-lined street leads off this square. Park and take the time to look around. There is normally a kiosk on or around the square selling freshly-made *gateau basque* (with cream or blackcurrant filling).

Leaving Sara, take the road which heads uphill from the square by Hotel Arraza, signposted GROTTES-LEZEA, and descend to a **mini-roundabout** just before the river (69km). (*Detour:* A 5km detour from this roundabout leads to the Caves of Sara, signposted 'Grottes Prehistoriques' (∩🚌3). On the way, there are many beautiful farmhouses, several of which are *chambres d'hôtes*. Short walk 3 for motorists, described on page 18, may be done in the reverse direction from here.)

From the mini-roundabout the main tour heads over the river bridge, still on the D4, towards AINHOA. Some 3km further on, turn right over the Nivelle River and then left on the D3905, a narrow country lane which meanders through a thick forest alongside a stream. When you reach the main D20 road, turn right and immediately you will find yourself on the main street of **Ainhoa** (77km ♦ ▲ ✕), lined with extremely colourful houses with wood-beamed façades. This is perhaps the most beautiful village of all in Lapurdi. The border is just 2km further south, at Dantxarinea (from where Zugarramurdi, described in Car tour 2, may be reached in 4km from the first roundabout after the customs post).

From Ainhoa this tour heads back along the D20, then turns right on the D918 to **Espelette** (83km ▲ △ ✕). From the first round-about, at the entrance to the village, head up the hill to the main, winding street, with more colourful half-timbered houses.

This is another pretty place, famous for its red peppers, which may be seen drying outside the houses. Continue through the village and turn right by the park on the D249 towards *ITXASSOU-ITSASU*.

Continue through **Itxassou** (89km 🔺△✕), past the main square, and turn right down a lane opposite a new, incongruous-looking indoor *frontón* called Trinquet Balaki. You will pass a signpost pointing to 'Hotel Restaurant Paradis' on your right. Turn left at the bottom of the hill and pass the church and the Hotel Restaurant du Chene, as you enter the **Pas de Roland** (❋). Having driven through rolling hills for a while on this tour, this narrow gorge now gives you the sensation of really being in the Pyrenees. The fast-flowing Nive River to the left is a popular rafting spot. The road is extremely narrow as it snakes through the gorge, but there are passing places. Park the car by the quaint little Hotel Restaurant Pas de Roland (92km 🔺✕🅿️P) and enjoy the glorious scenery by the river, which makes an ideal place to picnic and view the circular rock arch associated with the Roland legend. Walk 27 begins here.

Turn left over the bridge at Pas de Roland and follow the narrow lane beside the Nive. Take the next left turn (99km) and then turn right (101km) down towards the pretty collection of farmhouses scattered over the valley on the outskirts of Bidarrai. On reaching the valley floor about 300m further on, the lane to the right leads to the starting point for Walk 28, as well as picnic sites (🅿️P) along the Baztán River.

The main tour heads left here: cross the metal bridge, and turn left again to reach the old **Pont d'Enfer** over the Nive (102km). Continue past the hotel of the

Top: Pas de Roland; above: red peppers drying on a butcher's shop in Espelette

same name and up the hill to the pretty village of **Bidarrai** (⛪🔺✕), with its church and *frontón*. The famous **Iparla Ridge** may be climbed from behind the Aunamendi refuge in the corner of the square (see *Landscapes of the Pyrenees*).

Return to the **Pont d'Enfer** (104km), cross the new bridge and turn left on the main D918, then turn right on the same road to enter **Cambo-les-Bains** (117km 🔺△✕), where *Cyrano de Bergerac* was written. Turn right at

Pont d'Enfer at Bidarrai

the first roundabout, towards
HASPARREN. Just outside the town
there is an impressive **spa** with
ornate, Moorish-style gardens off
to the right. The road continues
through **Urcuray/Urkoi** (124km
✝) with its quaint little church and
cemetery. Walk 29 starts here.
Beyond the village, take a sharp
left (126km) up the hill before
Hasparren, heading for BAYONNE/
BAIONA. This is the start of the
D22, the **Route des Cîmes** (✳), a
pleasant route over the hilltops,
with panoramic views all around
and nicely off the beaten track.
Turn right on the D257 (140km)
towards MOUGERRE, to stay up on
the ridge. At the next main crossroads, go straight ahead up the hill
on the D712, to enter **Mougerre**
(143km ✝), a collection of more
wonderfully colourful half-
timbered houses along two
cobbled streets separated by a
beautiful church. This village is

perched on top of the highest hill
for miles around.
From here continue on to the
Croix de Mougerre (📷), a large
war memorial dedicated to victims
of the 1813-14 Napoleonic War.
From the car park on the right,
walk up to the memorial and
admire the view of the river Adour
and Bayonne/Baiona, with its twin-
spired cathedral clearly visible. The
G8 Adour-Pyrenées long-distance
footpath from Sara to Urt (on the
banks of the Adour to the north)
passes by here, and there is an
explanatory map in the car park.
Continue downhill on the D712
to the main road, turn right and
almost immediately you are on the
banks of the **Adour** (147km).
Turn left at the roundabout by the
river, to skirt alongside it. Once in
the old town (**Petit Bayonne**),
cross the bridge over the Nive and
return to the tourist office in
Bayonne/Baiona (151km).

Car tour 8: THE MOUNTAINS, FORESTS AND CANYONS OF XIBEROA

St Jean-Pied-de-Port/Donibane Garazi • Selva de Irati • Larrau • Logibar • Holtzarte Gorge • Kakueta Gorge • Santa Grazi/Ste-Engrâce • Arette • Tardets • Gotein • Mauleon • Bidouze River • St Jean-de-Port/Donibane Garazi

162km/101mi; about 4h15min driving time
En route: Short walks for motorists 18, 19; Walks 30, 31, 32
This route includes some mountain roads which may be snow-covered in winter — the road via the Chalets of Irati reaches 1327m, and the road above the small ski resort of Arette-la-Pierre-St Martin 1765m, although the latter road at least is usually kept open all year round. The detour to the start of Short walk 19 at the

Source de Bidouze involves a 3km drive on an unsurfaced, fairly potholed road, but it can be negotiated by normal vehicles.
Picnic suggestions: Lacs d'Iraty (28km); **Kakueta Gorge**, just before the waterfall (60km); **Arette River** (90km); at the end of lane leading to Short walk 19 to the **Source de la Bidouze** and also at the start of the walk itself, by the river (detours of 3.5km and 6.5km respectively from Donaixti Ibarre-St Just, the 140km-point)

T his tour covers some of the most intriguing landscapes of the Western Pyrenees, in particular the extraordinary canyon country around Santa Grazi/Ste-Engrâce. The province of Xiberoa also provides perhaps the best chance to observe rural Basque life in and around its small villages. Until fairly recently these pastoral settings were still a fairly isolated part of the French Basque Country. The tour starts in beautiful St Jean-Pied-de-Port/Donibane Garazi, a not-to-be-missed town.

St Jean-Pied-de-Port/Donibane Garazi (✝▲⛰△✕🚉) is a major departure point for the Pilgrims' Route to Santiago and a wonderfully preserved, colourful old town of cobbled streets full of character. Turn right from the **office de tourisme** along the main road heading out of town and follow signs towards the D933 and PAU at the first roundabout. At **St Jean-le-Vieux** (4km), turn right on the D18 towards IRATY. The road initially winds through farmland and a series of hamlets with great views ahead to the pointed summit of **Mt Behorlegy**. It then starts its steep climb (14km) up towards the Irati plateau, until it runs roughly parallel with the long, crescent shaped-ridge of Behorlegy, now on the far side of

the valley. (*Detour:* After 19km, a narrow lane descends to the right, to a beautiful, isolated valley below Mt Irau, a detour of 4km.) The main tour keeps ahead to the **Col de Burdinkurutz** (23km 📷), where the long ridge of Mendibeltza and Arthonatze meets the road. Descend to the **Chalet de Cize** (25km ✕) on the plateau. The **Selva de Irati** (✳) forms part of one of the largest forested areas in the Pyrenees. This chalet provides meals and refreshments, as do a couple of small, seasonally-opening huts. (*Detour:* A 1km detour from here leads past some ponds on the plateau to the end of the road at Chalet Pedro, from where the GR10 ascends to the cromlech-topped site of Okabe (🏔) up above the forest.)

47

Santa Grazi/Ste-Engrâce under a sprinkling of snow

From the Chalet de Cize, continue along the D18 to the **Lacs d'Iraty** (28km △🍴P). The second and smaller of the two lakes makes an especially pleasant picnic setting. From here the road climbs up higher into the Forest of Iraty, to a flat area where there is a collection of wooden chalets known as the **Chalets d'Iraty** (32km 🍴🏠). They are available to rent throughout the year and a cross-country skiing centre in winter. There are fantastic views from here to Mt Ori, the first Pyrenean peak over 2000m when travelling westwards from the Atlantic. Continue on down the mountain to the pretty village of **Larrau** (44km ♨🍴△🏠), perched on the hillside overlooking some impressive rocky crags. The road from here over the Pyrenees to Ochagavía in Nafarroa via the **Col de Larrau** is only reliably snow-free from May to October, but during these months it makes a good way to link up with Car tour 6. Descend through the village on the D26 to the bar/refuge of **Logibar** (46km) tucked into the

bottom of the valley. The GR10 passes through here, and Walk 30 to the hanging bridge of Holtzarte and its gorge starts from the car park behind the refuge.
Continue down the Larrau Valley and turn right (53km) towards SAINTE-ENGRACE. This is probably the most isolated valley remaining in the French Basque Country and one of its most beautiful. The road is narrow and winding as it follows the river past a small reservoir and a riverside campsite (△) to the entrance to the **Kakueta Gorge** (60km ❋🏠18).
Continue on past the pretty hamlets in the valley to **Santa Grazi/Ste-Engrâce** (630m; 64km ✝🏠). The 11th-century Romanesque church here has some extremely old discoidal steles in the graveyard. The terrace of the welcoming Auberge Elitchalt, opposite the church, makes an excellent rest stop, from where you can look out to the immense walls at the entrance to the Ehüjarre Canyon, setting for Walk 31.
The tour continues from here on the D113 up to the head of the

In the Kakueta Gorge

Short walk for motorists

🚍 18 Kakueta Gorge

*4.5km/2.8mi; 2h. This is the most
famous gorge in the French
Basque Pyrenees, 2km long and
over 350m deep in places. At its
narrowest, the walls are only 5m
apart. Although this is a very
popular tourist attraction (open
from 15/03 to 15/11; entrance
ticket € 4 from the Bar Cascade),
it's a beautiful walk. The lush
vegetation is more reminiscent of
tropical climes than the Pyrenees.
There is a waterfall towards the
end of the gorge, with pleasant
picnic spots nearby, and beyond it
is a cave.* Take care as you
negotiate the rocks and the plank
boardwalks, which can be slippery.
From the **Bar Cascade** descend
to the emerald-green waters of
the small **Bentia Reservoir** and
cross a second gorge on a footbridge. As you ascend on the far
side of the lake, the vegetation
thickens and explanatory boards
provide details of the wide
variety of lichens and other
plant life in the gorge. Descend
to the river on the other side of
the hill and pass through a
tunnel (15min). You now
enter the narrowest part of the
gorge, known as the **Grand
Etroit**, with its huge limestone
walls covered in moss. An
elevated boardwalk with railings
helps on slippery sections.
Cross the river just before some
rapids (30min) and rise gradually as the gorge widens out.
You come to a **waterfall
(45min)** which pours out of an
underground river emerging
from the rock face — a beautiful
spot to rest (⊼P) in view of the
falls. It is even possible to walk
right up behind the falls. The
path continues a further 200m,
up to a small grotto, which may
be entered (**1h**).
From here retrace your steps to
the **Bar cascade (2h)**.

valley, with fine views back to the
church at Ste-Engrâce. You enter
the **Forêt Comunal de Lanne** nd
climb to the **Col de Suscousse**
(1216m; 71km 📻). (*Detour:*
From this pass a narrow road to
the left leads to the cross country
ski resort of Issarbe.) The main
tour continues to a crossroads at
the **Col de Soudet** (1540m;
75km), just before the fairly small
ski resort of Arette-la-Pierre-St
Martin. (*Detour:* A right turn here
leads to the top of the pass on the
Spanish border at 1765m, for
Walk 32. The road continues to
the attractive Navarran villages of
Isaba and Roncal on the far side of
the pass.)
The main tour heads left from the
crossroads on the D132 towards
ARETTE. Once off the mountain
and on the valley floor, there are
several nice picnic sites (90km
⊼P) beside the road by the **Arette
River**. Continue on to **Arette**
(96km ⛰△✕🏠) and turn left by
the church. Drive through the
village on the D918 towards
LANNE and MAULEON. Another
mountain road leads back up to

St Jean-Pied-de-Port/Donibane Garazi

Issarbe (101km), but we continue through the pretty village of **Montory** to **Tardets** (110km 🏔✕🍴), with its attractive main square. (***Detour:*** A highly recommended 7km detour leads from the street on the right of this square, by the *office de tourisme,* to the hilltop chapel of La Madeleine (795m ✳✝🎦) via the extremely narrow and steep D347. It is a good idea to leave the car at the col about 1km before the chapel and walk up. There are twice-yearly pilgrimages to this site (on the Sunday before Easter and on July 22nd), and this is one of the best vantage points from which to view the high Pyrenees and the valleys of Xiberoa.)

The main tour continues from the square at Tardets on the main road towards MAULEON. It is worth stopping at **Gotein** (118km ✝△), to view the 16th-century church of **Saint André**, probably the best

example of the style of church typical of this region, with its *clocher trinitaire* and curious outside wooden staircase granting access to the upstairs pews (where the women traditionally sit — a custom still maintained today in these parts).

Carry on to the town centre of **Mauleon** (121km 🏨🏔✕🍴), the sleepy provincial capital of Xiberoa and the only town of any size in the province. Cross the river bridge and park in the large main square, to do a walking tour of **Vieux Mauleon** and the old hill-top castle. There is a helpful *office de tourisme* in the square, which can provide details of many walks in the area, as well as information about the *maskaradak* and *pastoralak,* plays and pageants performed and sung in Euskera which are unique to this area and which are held in the summer months. For the annual *pastoralak* (usually held at the end of July or early August), each village takes it in turn to go

on tour around Xiberoa with up to 70 participants.

Turn left at the end of the main square and follow the TOUTES DIRECTIONS sign to a roundabout and then head towards ST JEAN-PIED-DE-PORT on the D918. There are more great views over the valley from the **Col d'Osquich** (392m; 133km 📷), from where a 1km detour to the hilltop chapel of St Antoine is signposted. (***Detour:*** At 140km, just before Donaixti Ibarre-St Just, a lane to the left signposted SOURCE DE LA BIDOUZE descends to the Bidouze River. The asphalt ends after 3.5km by a farm and small picnic site (*⛩P*). From here it's another 3km on track to park by the footbridge where 🚗19 starts.)

The main tour continues on the main road from **Donaixti Ibarre-St Just** to the junction with the D933 (146km). Turn left here, back via **St Jean-le-Vieux**, to **St Jean-Pied-de-Port/Donibane Garazi** (162km).

Short walk for motorists

🚗 19 Source de la Bidouze

4km/2.5mi; 1h40min. This is a fairly short walk through the lower part of the Forêt d'Arbailles (Arbailleta), a beautiful and remote, unspoilt region of dense forest, to the extraordinary cave out of which the River Bidouze flows. The path involves crossing a couple of small streams, and the rocks on the approach to the cave are usually quite slippery, but this is otherwise an easy walk, with a total height gain of 350m. ***NB:*** *If you decide to leave your car at the farm where the asphalt ends, allow an extra 6km/1h30min for this walk. Otherwise follow the fairly potholed unsurfaced road for a further 3km from the farm, to a small footbridge and another small picnic site beside the river (350m;* ***⛩P****), still inside the forest.*

Cross the **footbridge** and follow yellow and scarlet marks on the rock, going uphill and further into the forest, gaining height above the river. Carry straight on where another path comes up from the river (**15min**). As you climb steadily, the route becomes more spectacular, as the path is carved out of the rock face and the river descends in a series of waterfalls (**25min**).

Cross a first stream and continue to follow yellow waymarking, ignoring a path to the left (**35min**). Go straight on at the next junction (**40min**) and *carefully* cross a second stream, strewn with large, moss-covered rocks (**45min**). When you come to a **cave** (650m; **50min**), go inside, to see the Bidouze emerging from its underground source and enjoy the view looking out at the dense forest in this magical place.

Then retrace your steps to the **footbridge** (**1h40min**).

Walking

The walks in this book have been carefully selected to offer as much variety as possible in terms of landscapes and level of difficulty. The Basque Country is blessed with many areas of outstanding natural beauty. All the walks are manageable for any reasonably fit person who is used to hill walking, and many involve relatively little gradient. Sections of walks which might demand a head for heights have been kept to an absolute minimum, and where possible an alternative route is given.

The longer, more strenuous walks featured on the following pages may be shortened in most cases; if so, shorter alternatives are mentioned in the 'logistics' section at the start of the walk. Access details are given for those travelling by car or public transport; for more public transport details, see the reverse of the touring map inside the back cover.

Maps

The maps in this book have been adapted from different sources, depending on the area covered. All maps are at at scale of 1:50 000, thus providing sufficient detail for the walker. Maps of the **Iparralde**/French Basque Country walks have been adapted from the French IGN 'Top 25' series, those of the three provinces of the **Comunidad Autónoma Vasca** are adapted from the Gobierno Vasco's 1:25 000 series, and those of **Nafarroa** from the Instituto Geográfico Nacional maps covering the whole of Spain (also at a scale of 1:25 000).

While there are five fold-out sheets which cover the whole of Iparralde (numbers 1245 ET, 1245 OT, 1345 ET, 1346 ET and 1346 OT), the Gobierno Vasco and Spanish IGN maps are sold as very small sheets, and over 200 maps are needed to cover the four provinces! A better bet is to obtain specific maps in the 'Cuadernos Pirenaícos' series, published by Sua Edizioak. These are very detailed, high quality, reasonably priced maps, on sale in local bookshops in the main towns. They also include booklets (in Spanish) outlining many walking routes.

Waymarking

The Basques themselves are keen walkers, and waymarking is in general of an extremely high standard. Firstly, there are the various GR routes crossing the region — long-distance footpaths on both sides of the Pyrenees, waymarked in red and white. These include the Trans-Pyrenean GR10 and GR11 crossing the entire Pyrenees from coast to coast (on the French and Spanish sides respectively) and the GR12 Sendero de Euskal Herria across the whole Spanish Basque Country. There are also relatively short GR routes, such as the three-day GR20 Vuelta de la Sierra de Aralar and the week-long GR121 Vuelta de Gipuzkoa.

There also short-distance PR and SL routes, which are waymarked in yellow and white and green and white respectively, which cover local areas.

Thirdly, there are many short trails waymarked in other colour combinations, details of which are usually given on information boards at the start of trailheads.

Many of the walking routes in this book follow sections of *all* the aforementioned types of footpath. In any case, all the walks described provide precise instructions, regardless of whether waymarking is adequate or not.

Where to stay

The Basque Country has an extensive network of reasonably-priced accommodation in rural areas. In the **Comunidad Autónoma Vasca**, the *agro-turismo/nekazalturismoa* (rural accommo-dation programme) extends to every corner of the region, and all local tourist offices stock a booklet containing a comprehensive list. You can also book such accommo-dation on the internet (www. nekatur.net). In **Nafarroa**, these are called *casas rurales/ landa etxeak* and, as the name implies, it is often necessary to rent a whole house rather than just a room. The Gobierno Foral de  Navarra publishes a comprehensive booklet detailing all accommodation in the province, again available through tourist offices or on the internet (www.cfnavarra.es/ turismonavarra). In **Iparralde**, there is an excellent choice of rural accommodation in the form of *gîtes* (www.gites-de-france.fr) and many small country hotels — the best source of information for the latter in the French Basque Country, many of which are grouped together as 'Logis de France', is via www.touradour.com/logis/LOGIHOTP.HTM. All the types of accommodation mentioned above are easily recog-nised by distinctive signs (the photograph above illustrates signposting in the Comunidad Autónoma Vasca).

Most towns of any size in the Spanish Basque Country,

especially those on the coast, also have an inexpensive, albeit at times fairly basic *casa de huésped*, *hostal* or *pensión*, recognisable by the signs CH, H and P respectively, and in the major tourist resorts such as Donostia-San Sebastián and Biarritz there is a variety of accommodation across the spectrum.

Further into the mountains, other options for walkers are: **on the French side**, *gîtes d'étapes* (www.gite-etape.com), usually located conveniently along the GR long-distance walking routes, notably the GR10 Trans-Pyrenean walk as it passes through the French Basque provinces. **On the Spanish side**, most mountain areas covered in this book (not just those in the Pyrenees) have a *refugio/aterpe*. These, and the *gîtes de'étapes* in France, are shown on the relevant walking maps and mentioned in the descriptions. It is always advisable, however, to phone in advance to check opening times if travelling out of season, even if the refuge concerned is supposed to be open year round. Finally, there are campsites in most areas of natural beauty in the region, details again being available through local tourist offices.

Weather

There is a **marked contrast in weather between the three distinct areas** comprising the Basque Country — those close to the coast, the high mountains, and the plains. The coastal region and immediate hinterland (and indeed the entire Atlantic coast of northern Spain and southwest France) is extremely green for good reason. It can rain at any time of year, and when it does, you can be in for a soaking. On the other hand, the region also enjoys a generally mild climate without extremes of temperature either in high summer or mid-winter. The plains (central and southern Nafarroa and Araba) are both physically and climatically an extension of Castile — in other words dry, with hot summers and harsh winters when the temperature drops below zero. The high mountains (including the Pyrenees and the interior of Gipuzkoa, Bizkaia, Iparralde and northern Nafarroa) may be snow-bound from November to April.

Essentially, **most of the walks in this book can be done at any time of year**, although mountain ranges like the Sierra de Aralar or Sierra de Urbasa may be covered with snow for some part of the winter. However, Walks 24, 25, 30, 31 and 32 may be out of bounds from November to April because of the risk of snow. Conversely, temperatures do not necessarily soar so high in mid-summer as to make walking really uncomfortable (except possibly in the more southern corners of the region, where Walks 16, 18, 19 and 23 are located). The Basques, who are renowned hearty eaters, tend to do their walking before lunchtime. Thus they avoid the hottest part of the day, and they descend or return to the nearest bar or restaurant in time for a huge lunch!

Clothing and equipment

The general rule is always to carry the minimum possible, without leaving any essentials behind. Decent walking boots, provided they have already been broken in, are required for many of the walks and indeed advisable for all of them, although sturdy shoes or good trainers may be enough for some of the more gentle coastal and forest walks. Where this is the case, mention is made in the introduction to the walks concerned. Raingear is also *essential,* as even on the sunniest of days, the weather can easily change, albeit in the form of a brief passing shower.

If you need to buy any equipment, there are excellent sports and camping shops in all major towns in the region, a good place to start being one of the branches of the Decathlon hypermarket chain, in Anglet (near Bayonne/Baiona), Donostia-San Sebastián, Bilbao or Iruña-Pamplona.

A basic checklist for day walks could be as follows:

small backpack	detachable trousers
water bottle	sunglasses
sun hat	sun cream
small first aid kit	compass
torch (for exploring caves)	waterproof/windproof (preferably
walking boots (broken in)	Goretex) jacket
mobile phone/emergency numbers	lightweight waterproof trousers
telescopic walking stick (also handy	gloves
for shooing away barking dogs)	penknife
insect repellent	food
fleece	binoculars

Dogs and other animals

The walker will invariably come in contact with **farm dogs**, as practically all Basque *baserri* have one tied up to warn their owners in good time of possible intruders. These will usually bark incessantly, but rarely do more than bark!

Sheepdogs need to be given a wide berth wherever possible, as they can be quite intimidating as they go about their duty looking after the flock. A decent stick is recommended to ward them off, and is an extremely useful piece of equipment for any walk. If dogs really worry you, Sunflower sells an ultrasonic 'Dog Dazer' (www.sunflowerbooks.co.uk).

Bulls fortunately do not tend to roam loose on mountainsides, and cows in the main are pretty docile. Nonetheless, I generally *avoid making direct eye contact* with **cows**, **horses**

Mt Txindoki (Walk 4), seen from the N1 on Car tour 1

or even **billy goats**, and will always try to respect their space if they happen to be on or near the path — certainly *it is important not to get between a young calf or foal and its mother.*

In 20 years of walking in the Basque Country I have never seen a **snake**, although vipers do exist. The biggest nuisances you will doubtless encounter are **flies**, **mosquitoes** and **midges**, especially in heavily forested areas, so it is important to carry an adequate supply of insect repellent.

Safety and responsible behaviour

For your own protection, please heed the following advice. Until you get used to the terrain, you can always start off by doing a couple of the short walks for motorists or a shorter section of one of the main walks.

- **Do not overestimate your ability**. Much of the Basque terrain is mountainous, and many of the walks described involve varying degrees of ascent/descent, sometimes on narrow paths. Read through the introduction to the walk, to get a general overview of its degree of difficulty. (In fact, it is always a good idea to read through the *whole* walk in advance!)
- Try to **avoid walking alone** if possible and/or inform a responsible person beforehand of your intended route.
- **Always keep an eye on the weather.** Local people who are familiar with the terrain, such as farmers and shepherds, are the best sources of information. A compass can be a life-saver if a mountain should suddenly become enveloped in mist.
- Make sure you have enough **warm clothing** for higher altitudes.
- If a route is different from that described or has become **unsafe** due, for instance to storm damage, be prepared to turn back.
- Ensure that you have **sufficient water** (1-2 litres per person) before the start of the walk — natural springs with drinking water are noted in the text, providing the chance for a refill, but it's best to set off with enough for the entire walk anyway.

- **Do not light fires.** Use camping stoves.
- **Do not frighten animals.** Keep dogs on a lead.
- **Walk quietly** through all farms, hamlets and villages, **leaving gates just as you found them.**
- **Stay on the path** wherever it exists, to minimise damage to surrounding vegetation. Don't take short cuts on zigzag paths; this hastens ground erosion.
- **Protect all wild and cultivated plants**.
- **Take all your litter away with you**.
- **Respect local bye-laws**, especially with reference to 'wild camping'. Always choose an unobtrusive site.
- **Keep well away from streams** when attending to 'calls of nature'. Do not use detergents for washing/washing-up.

Language hints

Castilian Spanish and French are universally spoken on their respective sides of the Pyrenees, but the Basque language (**Euskera**) is what most bonds the Basque people together, and any effort on the part of foreigners to learn a few phrases is much appreciated. Euskera has a standardised form known as *batua*, which is increasing in use and is taught in the schools, but there are still many discrepancies in terms of spelling (in particular between the Spanish Basque provinces and those of Iparralde). As a general rule, the further away you are from urban or tourist areas, the more Euskera you will hear spoken. Below are a few phrases to try out:

English	*Euskera*	*Approximate pronunciation*
Hello	Kaixo	**kai**-show
Goodbye	Agur	ah-**gore**
Good morning	Egun on	eh-goon-**on**
Good afternoon	Arratsalde on	ah-rats-**al**-deh-on
Good evening/ goodnight	Gabon	gab-**on**
How are you?	Zer moduz?	**sair**-mod-oos?
Fine, and you?	Ondo, eta zu?	**on**-doh, eh-tah-**soo**?
Please	Mesedez	meh-**seh**-dess
Thank you very much	Eskerrik asko mil esker	ess-keh-ree-**kas**-koh mil-es-**keh**
Not at all	Ez horregatik	ess-or-**reh**-gah-tik
How much is it?	Zenbat da?	**sen**-bat-da?
Yes	Bai	buy
No	Ez	ess
Where is...?	Non dago....?	**noon**-dah-goh?
Is this the way?	Hau da bidea?	**ow**-dah-bee-day-ah?
To the right	Eskubira	ess-**koo**-bee-rah
To the left	Eskerrera	ess-**keh**-reh-rah
Straight on	Aurrera	ow-**reh**-ra
Up	Goian	**goy**-an
Down	Behean	**bay**-an
I'm lost	Galduta nago	gal-**doo**-tah nah-goh

Glossary

Road signs tend to be in Spanish/Euskera or French/Euskera (and increasingly only in Euskera). Place names depend on the policy of individual town halls. In some cases, the official names of towns or cities may be double-barrelled (such as Donostia-San Sebastián), only in Euskera (such as Errezil) or most commonly referred to in Spanish or French (as is the case with Bilbao and Biarritz). *This book uses the most widely-used term in each case first,* followed by its equivalent in one of the two other relevant languages where necessary: for instance, St Jean-de-Luz/Donibane Lohizun.

The walker will come across many signs in Euskera on the routes described and on maps, so a basic vocabulary is useful. The letter *a* is added to nouns in order to form the definite article, unless the noun already ends in *a* (eg: *etxe* = house; *etxea* = the house); *k* is added to form the plural (*etxeak* = houses). Oft-recurring sounds are *tx* (pronounced like the *ch* in chat), *ts* (similar to *tx* but slightly softer), *tz* (pronounced like the *zz* in pizza) and *x* (pronounced like *sh* as in sheep).

Euskera	Approximate pronunciation	English
Aparkaleku	ah-**par**-ker-leh-koo	car park
Aran	ah-**ran**	valley
Aterpe	a-**tair**-peh	refuge
Atsedenleku	ah-**che**-den-leh-koo	picnic site
Baserri	**bah**-seh-ree	farmhouse
Berri	**beh**-ree	new
Bide	**bee**-deh	path
Borda	**bor**-der	(shepherd's) hut
Eliza	eh-**lees**-er	church
Enparantza	en-per-**antz**-er	square
Erdialde	air-dee-al-deh	town/city centre
Errota	eh-**roh**-ter	mill
Etorbide	eh-**tor**-bee-deh	avenue
Erreka	eh-**reh**-ker	stream
Errepide	eh-reh-**pee**-deh	(asphalted) road
Etxe	**eh**-cheh	house
Gailur	**guy**-loo-er	peak; summit
Gaztelu	**gas**-teh-loo	castle
Gurutz	**goo**-roots	cross
Haitz/Harri	aitz/**ah**-ree	rock; crag
Haritz/harizti	ah-**ritz**/ah-**ris**-tee	oak/oak grove
Harrespila	ah-res-**peel**-yah	cromlech
Herri	**eh**-ree	village; small town
Hilerri	ill-**yeh**-ree	cemetery
Hondartza	on-**darts**-er	beach
Ibai	ee-buy	river
Ikurriña	ee-koo-**ree**-nee-er	(the Basque) flag
Iparralde	ee-pah-**rahl**-deh	the French Basque Country
Iturri	ee-**too**-ree	spring
Jauregi	how-**reh**-gee	palace

Kale	**kah**-leh	street
Laku	**lah**-koo	lake
Landa etxe	**lan**-der **eh**-cheh	casa rural
Lauburu	lau-**boo**-roo	(the Basque) cross (a symbol seen everywhere)
Lepo	**leh**-poh	pass; col
Leze	**leh**-seh	cave
Mendi	**men**-dee	mountain
Mugarri	moo-**gah**-ree	boundary stone
Nekazalturismo	neh-kah-**sal**-tour-is-moh	agroturismo
Oihan	**oi**-ann	forest
Ostatu	oss-**tah**-too	inn
Pago/pagaldi	**pag**-oh(pag-**al**-dee)	beech/beech forest
Udal etxe	**oo**-dal **eh**-cheh	town hall
Uharte	oo-**ah**-teh	island
Sagardotegi	sag-**ar**-doh-tay-gee	cider house
Trikuharri	tree-koo-**ah**-ree	dolmen
Turismo bulegoa	tour-**is**-moh boo-**leg**-oh-ah	tourist office
Urjauzi	or-**how**-see	waterfall
Urtegi	or-**tay**-gee	reservoir
Zahar	**sah**-ar	old
Zubi	**soo**-bee	bridge

Getting about

The **Spanish Basque provinces** have a fairly extensive public transport system, enabling the walker to reach the start and end of many of the walks in this book, although sometimes a taxi is also required. The Spanish state rail system, *Renfe* (www.renfe.es) operates services in the provinces of the Comunidad Autónoma Vasca and Nafarroa on the main routes through the region, Irún to Donostia-San Sebastián and Bilbao to Vitoria-Gasteiz and Iruña-Pamplona. The most useful services for the walks included are the *trenes de cercanía,* local trains which stop at most stations, including request stops at minor halts.

A second rail system is operated by Euskotren (www. euskotren.es), which runs the routes primarily along the coast between Hendaye/Hendaia on the French side of the border and Donostia-San Sebastián, and from the latter via Zarautz, Zumaia and Durango to Bilbao, as well as routes serving the Bilbao conurbation and to Gernika and Bermeo. It also runs connecting bus services to certain points in Gipuzkoa.

Bus routes in the Spanish Basque Country are operated by a plethora of local companies. Companies running the routes between the provincial capitals (and to other parts of Spain) are Pesa (www.pesa.es), Continental Auto (www.continental-auto.es) and Alsa (www.alsa.es). In Bizkaia, most routes are covered by just one company —Bizkaibus (www.bizkaia.net). Elsewhere, the most useful services are generally run by small companies covering the more rural areas. Names, telephone numbers and relevant timetables are shown on the back of the fold-out map at the end of this book.

In the **French Basque Country**, the French state railway SNCF (www.ter-sncf.com) operates the main coastal route from Bayonne/Baiona to the border at Hendaye/Hendaia and also a useful, picturesque branch line from Bayonne/Baiona inland to St Jean-Pied-de-Port/Donibane Garazi, stopping at points fairly close to the start of Walks 27 and 28.

There are plenty of buses serving the relatively densely-populated French Basque coast between Bayonne/Baiona and Hendaye/Hendaia, mostly run by ATCRB, but services to the more rural areas inland are limited, the few existing being operated by small companies. In Lapurdi, two local bus companies, Le Basque Bondissant and Autocars Sarl Lata, are useful for Walks 26 and 29 respectively. But further into the mountains in the province of Xiberoa (Walks 30, 31 and 32), there is no public transport at all.

It is important to **check all timetables** shown for buses and trains, even though they were accurate at press date. It's a good idea to ask the relevant local tourist offices for up-to-date details, or to call the bus/train companies directly.

Another option is of course to **hire a car**, and this is easily done in all major towns in the Basque Country. In France, you will find rental firms at tourist centres such as Bayonne/Baiona, Biarritz and St Jean-de-Luz/Donibane Lohizun and in the provincial capitals of St Jean-Pied-de-Port/Donibane Garazi and Mauleon. In Spain, car hire is best arranged in one of the four provincial capitals: Bilbao, Donostia-San Sebastián, Vitoria-Gasteiz or Iruña-Pamplona.

Organisation of the walks

The 32 main walks in this book have been designed to link up with the eight car tours as follows:

Walks 1-5	Car tour 1
Walks 6-10	Car tour 2
Walks 11-13	Car tour 3
Walks 14-17	Car tour 4
Walks 18-22	Car tour 5
Walks 23-25	Car tour 6
Walks 26-29	Car tour 7
Walks 30-32	Car tour 8

When planning a walk, begin by looking over the fold-out map at the back of the book and noting which walk are closest to the part of the region you are touring, and then check the details of the relevant car tour. Detailed maps, as well as descriptions are given for each walk, and there is at least one

Larrun summit (Walk 26)

photograph showing a section of each walk, to give you an idea of the landscape.

Each walk has been carefully selected to include the most variety in terms of scenery. Wherever possible, routes are described so that most of the ascent is at the start of the walk. Many of the walks are circuits, although in the case of some mountain ascents, it is simply more practical to return along the same route. An effort has been made to ensure that starting points are as close as possible to public transport access, but often there will be a distance of a few kilometres to the nearest bus stop or train station. In the remote mountainous areas, however, and in particular in inland Iparralde (the French Basque Country), public transport is simply non-existent!

Each walk begins with information on 'logistics': distance in kilometres and miles, approximate walking time, grade (including the quality of waymarking), and access. Where walks are accessible by bus or train, the relevant timetables are provided on the back of the large fold-out map, together with phone numbers and/or websites of the bus/railway companies (timetables should nonetheless always be re-checked beforehand, as changes inevitably occur). Below the 'logistics' is a brief summary of the attractions to be seen along the way.

Walking times given are those I calculated walking at a slow to average pace, and ***do not allow for stops at the points of interest described***, even mountain summits. Be sure to increase walking times by *at least* a third. Invariably, most walks will last a full day if weather conditions are optimum and you stop to picnic, swim, or take photographs!

The following symbols are used on the walking maps:

▬▬▬	motorway	↔	spring, waterfall, etc	⋔	prehistoric site
▬▬▬	trunk road	⸸	church, monastery	∩∩	cave.aqueduct
▬▬▬	secondary road	⸸	chapel	△	campsite
▬▬▬	minor road	†	cross	■	specified building
▬▬▬	motorable track	▲	summit marker	⸸	refuge
▬▬▬	other track	⇥	cemetery	⛪	*agroturismo*
─ ─ ─	cart track, path, trail	⊼	picnic site	✳	mill
$\overset{2\rightarrow}{=}$	main walk	🖾	viewpoint	⌁	rock formation.cairn
$\overset{2\rightarrow}{=}$	alternative walk	🚌	bus stop	ⓘ	monument, tower
🚗8	walk for motorists	🚉	railway station	*i*	tourist office
─ 400 ─	height in metres	🚗	car parking	⌇	electricity substation
		■□	castle, fort.ruins	⋏	communications mast

Walk 1: GROS BEACH • SAGÜES • CLIFF-TOP WALK AROUND MT ULIA • ILLURGITA • AQUEDUCT • FUENTE DEL INGLES • FARO DE LA PLATA • PASAI SAN PEDRO HARBOUR

Distance: 7.5km/4.7mi; 2h30min
Grade: moderate, with a fairly steep 250m ascent from Gros Beach to Ulia at the beginning of the walk. The route then undulates along the cliff tops. The descent to the harbour of Pasai San Pedro is also fairly steep. The route is very well waymarked in red and white,

forming part of the GR121 vuelta de Gipuzkoa.
Equipment: see page 55; decent trainers are fine.
Access: the walk starts in the city centre of Donostia-San Sebastián, by the tourist office, C/Reina Regente No. 3, returning to the city by 🚌 from Pasai San Pedro.

This walk provides an excellent chance to gain access to one of the best stretches of rugged coast, with the advantage of being right on the city's doorstep. The path hugs the clifftops for much of the route, meandering around the side of the heavily forested Mt Ulia. The approach to the lighthouse and the descent to the narrow channel granting access to the harbour of Pasaia are further highlights.

To start the walk turn left outside the **tourist office**, cross the bridge over the **Urumea River**, pass the Kursaal building and walk along the promenade of **Gros Beach**. At the far end of the beach, in the part of town directly below Mt Ulia known as **Sagüés**, follow the main road past the **church** and, just before the **petrol station**, turn left up **Zemoria Kalea**. Steps directly opposite provide a shortcut up the hill, to where the road ends in a cul-de-sac at the base of the hill (**20 min**). From here it's a short but steep climb of 250m up the steps to a lane on the hillside, from where you have a panorama of the whole city and its three beaches.

Turn left on the lane. After about 100m it peters out into a path cut between the hedgerows. Follow a path to the left marked 'LITORAL', which leads to the headland beyond Gros Beach and the 18th-century fortifications of **Monpás**. After being abandoned, these interesting ruins became a refuge for smugglers, who were very active along this coast.
The main route heads straight on and, after briefly ascending through a pine forest, emerges on the **clifftops** (**40min**). The path takes a sharp turn to the left beside the small spring of **Fuente Kutraia** (**45min**) and enters a narrow ravine; this cobbled section is a particularly pretty

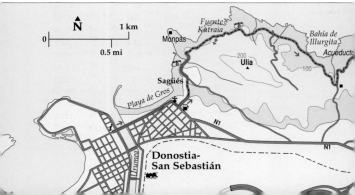

View over to Pasai Donibane from Pasai San Pedro

stretch, veering to the right and winding its way up to the highest point on this part of the cliffs (**1h**). From here the Plata Lighthouse may be seen in the distance, and the view extends well beyond — to Cape Higuer on the French border. The path crosses a road and drops towards the attractive cove of **Illurgita**, backed by lush vegetation. This makes a pleasant rest stop — just make your way through the bushes to the shore (**1h20min**). From here the route climbs towards a large school building on the hillside of **Mt Ulia** — a reminder of how near we still are to the city — and then continues to the left towards the lighthouse, past the remains of an old **aqueduct** and another spring, the **Fuente del Inglés** (**1h50min**), which supplied water to the city in the 19th century.

The road is reached at the **Faro de la Plata** ('Silver Lighthouse'; **2h**), perched high above the narrow,

treacherous channel granting access to the port of Pasaia. Around it and across the channel on the Mt Jaizkibel side, the sandstone cliffs form fascinating honeycomb shapes.

Turn right along the road (closed to traffic) and take the path to the left leading to a small **picnic site** (**⊨P**) with superb views of the channel, the whole port and the crags of Aiako Harriak in the distance. Some recently-built steps have much improved what used to be a very slippery path, but exercise caution after heavy rain nevertheless. Make your way down to a second, smaller **lighthouse** at sea level (**2h10min**), guarding the entrance to the channel. A pleasant promenade leads to the beginning of the built-up area and the landing place for the shuttle ferry across to the attractive fishing village of Pasai Donibane, directly opposite.

To end the walk, take the narrow street to the right (by a small **shrine**), into the old town of **Pasai San Pedro**. Walk past the **church** and on to the main road and **bus stop** (**2h30min**), where buses leave every 15 minutes for Calle Oquendo, beside the María Cristina Hotel in Donostia-San Sebastián and just two minutes' walk from our starting point.

63

Walk 2: BESABI • MONTEFRIO • ARROYO DE SOROTXOTA • MENHIR DE ETENETA • ADARRA • MATALE • BESABI

Distance: 7km/4.4 mi; 2h45min
Grade: moderate, fairly gradual ascent of 500m to Mt Adarra, returning down a steeper, more direct route. The route is not waymarked but mostly clear.
Equipment: see page 55
Access: 🚗 Follow Car tour 1 on the N1 to JUNCTION 447B, take the GI131 towards URNIETA and after a further 3.5km, when the road reaches the top of the hill at the **Alto de Irurain**, turn right by the Zelai Asador restaurant along a non-signposted lane which ends after 4km at the Bar/Restaurant **Besabi** (19.5km; car park).
🚌 G2 (Andoain-Urnieta bus, from Calle Oquendo, beside the María Cristina Hotel in Donostia-San Sebastián). Get off at **Alto de Irurain** just after the petrol station and walk 4km left up the lane mentioned above to Besabi. Or alight in the main street in Urnieta (1km before the petrol station), from where a taxi can take you to the **Bar Besabi**.

A darra is the closest mountain to the city of Donostia-San Sebastián and a popular walk — not only because it is so easily accessible but for the variety of landscapes it offers. The circuit described here combines a beautiful forest walk, Neolithic remains and fantastic views of the surrounding mountains and coast from the twin crags of Adarra's summit.

Start the walk from Bar/Restaurant Besabi, a very popular place with locals, especially on Sundays when the restaurant quickly fills up and walkers sit outside eating *bocadillos*. Take the asphalted lane to the left that heads steeply up the hill to the **Montefrio** farm, now an *agroturismo* (**5min**). Go through the gate opposite the farm — this first section is often quite muddy, due to its being a thoroughfare for walkers and farm animals alike. Follow the fence to the right. Take the next fork left, onto a stonier path, go through another **gate** (**10min**) and enter a pine forest. Pines soon give way to twisted beech trees as the forest becomes more dense, and the path starts to level out, veers to the right and crosses a small stream. On reaching the **Arroyo de Sorotxota** (**30min**), the main stream descending from Adarra, cross by making your way over the rocks, then take the path diagonally opposite. This zigzags further up above the beech forest, to a **clearing** (**35min**), where the twin crags of Adarra are to your left. Cross the clearing and take the path which gradually gains height, keeping the rocky outcrops of Adarra to your left all the way and the tree line just to your right. After circling Adarra, the path flattens out as it reaches some **pastureland** (**55min**). From this point, with the forest still to your right, follow the grassy path as it dips down to another small stream and then rises to the ridge and the **Menhir de Eteneta** (**1h05min**). This is one of the most striking Iron Age relics in the Basque Country, beside which is also a well-preserved **cromlech**, one of several in this area.

To ascend Adarra, go back along the ridge, aiming for the right of the two crags. The way is considerably less steep on this side of the mountain. The top of **Adarra** (811m; **1h30min**) affords great views in all directions. Take

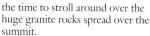

the time to stroll around over the huge granite rocks spread over the summit.

Then, keeping the bay of Donostia-San Sebastián directly in front of you in the distance, descend the steep grassy spur towards a pass between Adarra and the smaller outcrop of **Aballarri**. This is an exhilarating part of the hike. As you descend, look out for another, smaller **cromlech** to your right. When you reach a fence, keep it on your left until you arrive at the pass, the **Collado de Matale**. Now cross the fence and make for a *borda* in the shady area of beech trees shown above, where a couple of rustic **tables** (⊓*P*; **2h05min**) make a nice spot for a rest. From here the path descends further into the forest, rejoins the Arroyo de Sorotxota, and reaches the point where we crossed the stream earlier (**2h15min**). From here retrace your steps to Montefrio and **Bar Besabi** (**2h45min**).

Above, right: rustic picnic table on the woodland descent from Adarra.
Left: curiosities on the Adarra (top) and Ernio (bottom) summits. Many of the summits in the Spanish Basque Country are decorated with 'dolls' houses'. These are used as mailboxes, primarily by members of mountaineering clubs. People leave their names, and the name of their club, to prove that they've been to the top.

65

Walk 3: ALKIZA • ITXURAIN • IRUMUGARRIETA • ZELATUN • ERNIO • ZELATUN • ALKIZA

Distance: 13km/8mi; 4h30min
Grade: fairly strenuous, with an ascent of 700m from Alkiza to the summit of Ernio and some quite steep sections; otherwise fairly level walking. A longer, alternative circuit returning along the ridge of Ernio (see page 69) involves a similar 700m steep descent to Ernialde, although the path is at all times clear and safe. Waymarked in yellow and white from Alkiza to Zelatun, following the PR-GI78.
Equipment: see page 55
Access: 🚗 Follow Car tour 1 on the N1 to JUNCTION 439, then take the GI3650 signposted to IRURA and ANOETA. Go through Irura and on to **Anoeta** and turn right (21km) over the railway bridge. Then turn right again on the GI3630 to the small hilltop village of **Alkiza** and park in the village square (26km). 🚌 and 🚐 There are frequent trains from Donostia-San Sebastián main station to **Anoeta** (one stop before Tolosa). Walk up into the village and turn right about 100m along, on the road to Alkiza. The bus stop for **Alkiza** is beside the bridge over a stream.

Ernio is one of the most visited mountains in the Basque Country and with great justification. It's easily accessible from the coast, involves a very pleasant walk up through beautiful forest interspersed with open views over coast and mountains, a cosy refuge serving food, a spectacular final ascent along a beautiful stone path, a summit covered with giant crosses and the possibility of extending the walk along the entire ridge. This itinerary from Alkiza is one of the lesser known routes up Ernio — not the shortest, but the most varied.

First take the time to look over the beautiful valley below from the main square in **Alkiza** (340m), then **start the walk**: head back a few metres along the road to Anoeta, then take the first lane on the right (signposted 'ASKANTXO'). Pass **Lete** *baserri* on the right (now an *agroturismo*) and then take the first right turn beyond the village, along an asphalted lane signposted to ZELATUN (**5min**). After a large *baserri* (**10min**), the lane veers steeply to the left and becomes a farm track, gaining altitude as it climbs above the wooded **gorge** to your left. At the next crossroads (**25min**), leave the track and take the path to the right — a large **beech tree** stands about 20m directly in front of you. Gaining further height, the path emerges on a grassy mountain spur from where there are splendid views to the right as well as the one to your left. Go through a **gate** (**30min**) and enter a pine forest.

After a period of flat walking, the path climbs fairly steeply again, passes through another gate and emerges up on the hillside at the **Collado de Itxurain** (680m; **50min**). Just to your left are the remains of a **tumulus**. Continue straight ahead, now along the track you left earlier. The long ridge of Ernio now looms closer as we re-enter the forest. At the next **signpost** (**1h**), continue towards ZELATUN and very soon fork left uphill, following the yellow and white waymarking, heading deeper into the forest, as the path runs alongside the base of Ernio. Encircle a large **hollow** with some interesting limestone rocks and beautiful beech trees (**1h15min**) and follow the signpost to the **Collado de Irumugarrieta** (770m; **1h30min**), in a clearing above the tree line. This marks the border between four parishes. From here the path winds around the remainder of the north face of Ernio, with superb views towards the sea and the limestone strata of Mt Gazume.

You rise to the **Collado de Zelatun** (850m; **1h45min**), where there is a rustic but well-equipped **refuge** (open weekends throughout the year and every day from May to September; serves

View to the Ernio summit from the Collado de Zelatun

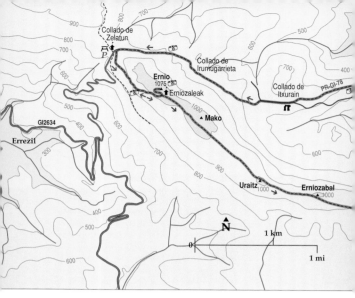

food; tel: 680-881206/659-702161) and **picnic site** (⚹*P*). Overlooked by the steepest, most abrupt face of Ernio, this pass is a major junction for walking routes over the mountains in the area. It is possible to drive up to the refuge on a very narrow and steep, rough road from **Errezil** (see Car tour 1), but this is not encouraged or advised.

Our trail to the summit of Ernio continues behind the refuge and climbs around the southern side of the mountain. In some places steps have been carved into the rock. As you ascend, the views of the valley far below and the village of Errezil

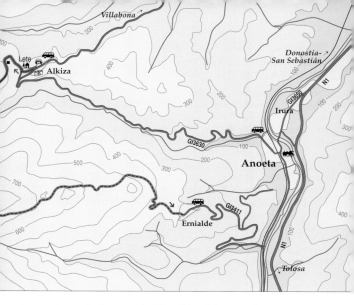

become increasingly dramatic. The trail, hugging the mountain all the way, ascends to a small refuge called **Erniozaleak** ('Friends of Ernio'; **2h15min**), a very welcome place to shelter if the weather changes. In front of this refuge is the first of the **many crosses**.

Turn left and make your way up to the summit of **Ernio** (1075m; **2h20min**), the top of which is covered with crosses of all different sizes, the oldest dating back to 1855. The inscriptions are all in Euskera. This is an important pilgrimage site for Basques and the *romerías* held every Sunday in September attract many people from the surrounding area.

Enjoy the impressive views on all sides before descending again to **Erniozaleak** and retracing your steps via **Zelatun** and Itxurain to **Alkiza** (**4h30min**).

Alternative return: From Erniozaleak you have the option of continuing along a path close to the top of the ridge, via the peaks of **Mako, Uraitz** and **Erniozabal**, all at around a height of 1000m, before dropping steeply to the village of **Ernialde**, where you could catch the Alkiza bus in the afternoon or walk a further 3km downhill to Anoeta. Allow 3h from the summit of Ernio to Ernialde.

Some of the crosses and memorials on the summit of Ernio; see also the bottom photograph on page 65

Walk 4: LARRAITZ • ORIA ITURRIA • BORDAS DE ZIRIGARATE • EGURRAL • TXINDOKI • EGURRAL • MUITZE • LARRAITZ

See also photograph page 56
Distance: 13km/8mi; 5h30min
Grade: strenuous, with an ascent of 946m. But whole families do this walk! The entire upward route — fairly gradual until the Oria Spring — is along a very well-used path. The final 200m of ascent from Collado Egurral to the summit is steep. Take care on the descent back to this pass, as the rocks can be slippery, although no scrambling is involved and the path is not overtly exposed. The descent via Muitze is safe, but the path is considerably narrower, and after heavy rain it may be advisable to descend to Larraitz via the ascent route. In clear, dry weather, however, the descent via Muitze, along a beautiful, little-used path is highly recommended.
Equipment: see page 55
Access: 🚗 Follow Car tour 1 to **Larraitz** (40km). Park in the large car park for the **Zamaoko Atsedenlekua** picnic site.
🚌 frequent buses and trains from Donostia-San Sebastián to **Tolosa**. From Tolosa take a bus to **Abaltzisketa**, then walk 1km along the road to Larraitz. (On Sundays, one bus continues to Larraitz in the morning, returning late afternoon.)

Txindoki is perhaps the most striking mountain in the Basque Country, with its classic Matterhorn-like shape. The summit, which is the end point of the Sierra de Aralar, offers incredible views over the entire region. This interesting circuit ascends via the usual, popular route from Larraitz around the south side of the peak and returns on a beautiful yet relatively little-used path via the Muitze Waterfall and the north face of the mountain.

Larraitz (400m), nestling below the north face of Txindoki, has an extremely popular picnic site as well as three bar/restaurants that fill up quickly at weekends, but which are good places to procure substantial *bocadillos* for the walk up to the summit. **Start the walk** from the far end of the car park for the **Zamaoko Atsedenlekua picnic site** (🚏*P*): go through a gate and follow the track. Ignore the lower track (**15min**) straight on to the smaller, neighbouring mountain of **Gaztelu** (with a similar, but less pronounced pointed summit), and keep left uphill. A short-cut **path** on the left (**20min**)

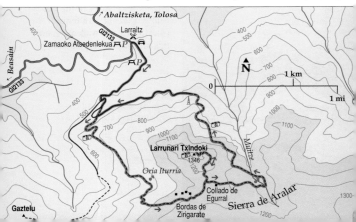

Top: Txindoki summit; bottom: borda *at the start of the Aralar plateau*

cuts off a bend. When you rejoin the track, turn right to head around the south side of Txindoki (the track to the left is your return route). As the path levels out and rounds a bend (**40min**) there are wonderful views towards Gaztelu in front of you, the long ridge of Aitzkorri beyond and the sheer rock face of Txindoki to the left. After passing through a gate and keeping the **pine forest** to your right, ascend around the mountain to **Oria Iturria** (**1h05min**), a spring where you can refill your water bottle. Once the path reaches the head of the valley and passes through another **gate** (**1h15min**) it zigzags more steeply up to the edge of the plateau of the **Sierra de Aralar**, a beautiful unspoilt range of undulating green pastureland and limestone peaks lying between 1000m and 1400m. Veering left and passing through another gate (**1h30min**), the path traverses an area of limestone rocks, hollows and *bordas* known as **Zirigarate**, until it reaches some **large rocky outcrops** (**2h05min**) just before the grassy spur of **Collado de Egurral** (1160m; **2h10min**). From here it is a steep climb up to the summit. The path is clear, although in some places quite eroded; yellow arrows on the rocks mark the way throughout. The last 100m or so are over rocks, but no scrambling is required. From the summit of **Txindoki** (1346m; **2h45min**), you can peer down to Larraitz almost 1000m directly below you, and on a clear day the view stretches to the sea and well towards the Pyrenees.
Descend the same way to back to **Egurral Pass** (**3h15min**), but then head left, down through the **grass gully** behind a *borda*. Ignore other paths to the left and right

and follow the course of a **small stream** fairly steeply down this gully until it enters the larger **Muitze Stream** (**3h35min**). Cross the stream and follow the path on the right towards the base of the **rock face** in front of you, passing through another **gate** (**3h40min**), from where the valley is visible far below. The path takes a sharp left and descends to the base of the **Muitze Waterfall** (**3h55min**). Cross the stream below it and proceed along a fairly narrow path cut into the rock face of Txindoki. Exercise caution on descending, although the path should not present any problems for vertigo sufferers, as the few exposed sections near the beginning are quite wide and safe. This entire descent, which follows the forested north face of Txindoki, provides fine views of the valley below. Descend to a **fence** (**4h40min**) and walk alongside this until you emerge beside a large **TV aerial** (**4h55min**). You go through a gate and join a grassy track. From here your starting point is directly below you, to the right, and looks very close, but follow the grassy track back to your ascent path (**5h15min**). Then retrace your steps to the car park at **Larraitz** (**5h30min**).

Walk 5: ALDAOLA • SAN ADRIÁN REFUGE • SAN ADRIAN TUNNEL • MT AITZKORRI • MT AKETEGI • MT AITXURI • ARBELAR • URBIA REFUGE • OLTZA • CALZADA ROMANA • SAN ADRIAN TUNNEL • SAN ADRIAN REFUGE • ALDAOLA

See also cover photograph
Distance: 16km/10 mi; 7h
Grade: strenuous, with a steep climb of 500m from the San Adrián Tunnel to the summit of Aitzkorri (which at least is done early on in the walk), and a short scramble to the top of the highest peak, Aitxuri. The return involves a slight gain in altitude from the Urbia Refuge but in general is a fairly gradual descent. All paths used are well defined and clearly waymarked. Allow a whole day for the complete circuit, especially if walking the additional 5km each way from Otzaurte Halt or descending to Arantzazu. Shorter options are: a return hike up to the San Adrián Tunnel and/or beyond it along the Calzada Romana (1h30min-2h) or a return walk to Aitzkorri, the first and most-visited peak (4h).
Equipment: see page 55
Access: 🚗 Follow Car tour 1 to Ordizia and continue along the N1 to JUNCTION 416, then turn left on the GI2637, signposted to

SEGURA and ZEGAMA. *Do* stop in the historic village of **Segura**, to see the old mansions on its main street and the pretty square. Follow signs through **Zegama** towards ALTSASU. When the road reaches the top of the pass, turn right opposite the **Venta de Otzaurte** along a narrow lane signposted to ATZANIKO ATSEDEN-LEKUA. After a further 2km, you pass the attractive **Beunde picnic site** (🪑P), with great views towards Mt Aratz ahead and the ridge of Aitzkorri to the right. Continue for a further 2km, until you reach a large stone at a point known as **Aldaola**, where a track leads off to the right. There is an explanatory map and information about walks in the area here. Park as near to here as you can — if there is no space, drive about 100m further on, to where there is more parking space on the right.
🚂: One early-morning train leaves daily from Donostia-San Sebastián main station to the **Apeadero de Otzaurte**, on the main line to Vitoria-Gasteiz. From the station, walk 100m to the road and turn right uphill to reach the the **Venta de Otzaurte**, from where you must walk an additional 4.5km to **Aldaola** along the route described above. An interesting option for those using public transport is to continue from the Urbia Refuge down to **Arantzazu Monastery**, where there is plenty of accommodation and you may be able to hitch a ride — or else walk down to the attractive historic town of **Oñati**, from where there are buses back to Donostia-San Sebastián.

Visit historic Segura village if you are driving to this walk.

This is a fairly long but extremely beautiful circuit. It visits the fascinating San Adrián Tunnel and takes in the well-preserved Calzada Romana (Roman Road; historically used as a link on the Pilgrims' Route to Santiago). You ascend through extensive beech woods to Mt Aitzkorri and walk along its ridge to Mt Aitxuri, the highest peak in the Basque Country outside the Pyrenees. At the Urbia Refuge you're surrounded by a typically verdant, high-meadow landscape.

Start the walk at **Aldaola**: follow the track behind the stone and turn left almost immediately (just before a **cattle grid**), to climb steeply up through woodland (red and white waymarking). Rejoin the same track higher up (**10min**); the San Adrián tunnel is now clearly visible in front of you on the mountain, and you reach the **San Adrián Refuge** (900m; **15min**; open all year; food and beds; tel: 943 582076). Fill up your water bottle from the spring just behind the building and continue along the trail behind it, rising gradually to the **San Adrián Tunnel** (1010m; **30min**). The **Chapel of Sancti Spiritus** inside this natural tunnel was originally used as a hospital for pilgrims. After passing through the tunnel you come upon the first stretch of the old **Calzada Romana**, with

Above: on the approach to the San Adrián Tunnel; left: woodland path to the Aitzkorri summit

well preserved paving. Just beyond the tunnel, veer right, away from the *calzada* (**35min**), following the yellow markings and sign to AITZKORRI.

The path climbs steeply up through dense beech forest, to emerge high on the mountainside at the start of a narrow path cut into the limestone (**1h30min**; see cover photograph). This path ascends steeply to the first of many **crosses** (**1h40min**), from where the village of Zegama is clearly

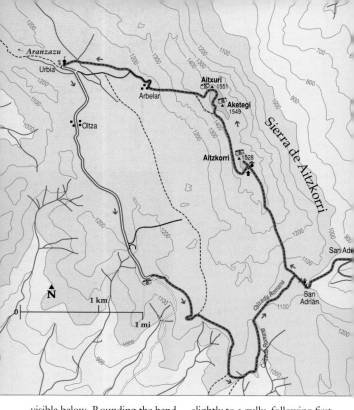

visible below. Rounding the bend, the chapel and refuge of Aitzkorri come into view. From here an exhilarating short ridge walk and final climb bring us to the summit of **Aitzkorri** (1528m; **2h05min**). The chapel is built just at the edge of the abyss, separated by a railing protecting walkers from a sheer 1200m drop to the valley below. From the summit, descend to the **chapel** (the interior of which is accessed by a dark passageway), and follow the path round to the right. Still waymarked in yellow, the path then contours slightly below the ridge itself. At a bend in the path (**2h35min**), just before it starts to descend towards the meadows of Urbia, some fairly faded markings show the way up the hillside on a small path to the second peak, **Aketegi** (1549m; **2h45min**). From here descend

74

slightly to a gully, following first yellow markings (**2h55min**) and then red markings up over the rocks to **Aitxuri** (1551m; **3h**), the highest point. This last peak involves a slight scramble over the rocks, but the vestiges of a path will guide you. Return to the gully and follow the red markings steeply and directly down the hillside to rejoin the main path (**3h20min**).

Descend to the collection of red-roofed *bordas* called **Arbelar** (**3h55min**; simple meals usually available here in summer), and proceed along the track. Then veer right, away from the track: follow a line of trees which forms a natural avenue, leading you to the **Urbia Refuge** (1136m; **4h30min**; open all year; food and beds; tel: 943 781316/943 585030), surrounded by the verdant high

Aitzkorri from Zegama

meadows bearing the same name. Another spring provides a chance to refill water bottles. (Option for those using public transport: from here a well-trodden path descends to the Arantzazu Monastery in 1h15min.)

To begin the return journey to Aldaola, follow the gravel road in front of the refuge, keeping the Aitzkorri Ridge to your left. Pass the *bordas* of **Oltza** (**4h55min**), descend to a stream and, just after a curious **natural hollow** where a stream disappears into a cave under the road, fork right uphill (**5h05min**). Continue until you see more red and white markings (**5h25min**), then follow the waymarked path to the left. This meanders in and out of the beech forest. At a **small clearing and hollow** (**5h50min**), forming a kind of natural 'roundabout' in the middle of the woods, *ignore* the red and white markings to the left (back to Urbia). Follow the red and white waymarked path straight ahead: this descends and eventually reaches the beginning of the **Calzada Romana**. Turn left and almost immediately reach a junction with **signposts**. (**6h10min**). Take the route marked SAN ADRIAN, to descend the best-preserved section of the *calzada* through the forest, back to the junction with the Aitzkorri path and the **San Adrián Tunnel** (**6h30min**). Go through the tunnel and retrace your steps past the **San Adrián Refuge** (**6h45min**), to the cattle grid. Turn right here, back to **Aldaola** (**7h**).

75

Walk 6: ESKAS • ELIZMENDI PATH VIA ERROIARRI WATERFALL • ARTIKUTZA VILLAGE AND RESERVOIR • OLD RAILWAY LINE • BALCON NATURAL • ESKAS

Distance: 9.5km/5.9mi; 3h30min
Grade: moderate. The walk descends gradually through the forest to Artikutza and, after a fairly steep climb of about 1km back up through the forest, follows the route of the former forest railway line. Waymarked throughout in yellow and white, following the PR-NA 124 to Artikutza and returning on the PR-NA 125. Overall ascents of 300m.
Equipment: See page 55
Access: 🚗 Follow Car tour 2 to the roundabout just beyond the Oiartzun motorway exit, where you turn right initially towards UGALDETXO. Then take the GI3631 towards ARTIKUTZA. This winding

scenic road ascends via **Collado de Uzpuru**, a small picnic site with fine views (12km 🍽*P*) and **Bianditz** (710m) to **Eskas**, the entry gate and guard's house for the **Artikutza Forest Reserve** (16km from the motorway exit). Park just before the gate. (To continue beyond the gate by car to Artikutza, special permission must be obtained from the town hall in Donostia-San Sebastián.) 🚌 from Plaza de Gipuzkoa in Donostia-San Sebastián to the main square in **Oiartzun**, from where a taxi can be taken to **Eskas** (13km).
NB: A map of the whole reserve may be purchased from the forest guard's house.

This walk offers the chance to see some of the densest forests of wild pine, oak and beech in the Basque Country, just forty minutes' drive from one of its major cities. Added attractions are the beautiful Erroiarri Waterfall deep in the forest, the unspoilt village of Artikutza and its neighbouring reservoir, and an interesting return walk along an old railway line through one of the higher parts of the forest — affording open views over the Artikutza basin.

Start the walk at **Eskas** (650m): go through the **gate** and follow the sign down the road towards ARTIKUTZA. Take the first path to the left (**5min**; signposted to ARTIKUTZA), beside an explanatory board about forest wildlife. This path, called '**Elizmendi**', plunges deep into a beautiful forest, mainly oak and beech. Beyond a couple of **twisted beech trees** (**20min**) the path descends to a first stream, crosses it by a rickety old **wooden bridge** (**35min**), follows the stream and then crosses a **second bridge** (**40min**). Soon after, take a path to the right (signpost: URJAUZIA-CASCADA). This leads to a viewpoint above the **Erroiarri Waterfall** (**45min**). A path to the right of the viewpoint descends to

a point just above the waterfall, where the crystal-clear water makes a wonderfully refreshing rest stop in the heart of the forest. Returning to the main path, continue through the forest; the path narrows and gains height above the river, before beginning its descent towards the reservoir. On reaching a gravel road and **signposts** (**1h30min**), a left turn marks the start of the SL-NA121 circuit of 6km around the **Enubieta Reservoir** (add an extra 1h30min, if you do this). The main walk turns right, through a gate. Fork right again along the asphalted lane, to pass the **church** and enter the village of **Artikutza** (315m; **1h40min**). The village itself consists of a few colourful,

Artikutza: the oak and beech wood (left) and the village (below)

ramshackle old *baserri* and a *frontón*; there are plenty of picnic tables (⊟P), and spring water beside the river. The handful of residents in this idyllic village are involved in forestry and livestock farming, and the reservoir constitutes the main water supply for Donostia-San Sebastián. Cross the main bridge opposite the *frontón*, following the sign 'ESKAS TRENBIDITIK', and proceed along the road past the **Ostatu Zahar** (a small refuge). Take the first path to the right, signposted to ESKAS (**1h50min**). This climbs fairly steeply, initially parallel to the road, and then runs deeper into the forest. Continue following signs to ESKAS at the next junction, which marks the start of the **old railway line** (BURNBIDE ZAHARRA-REN BIDEA/ CAMINO DEL ANTIGUO FERROCARRIL; **2h15min**). There are few traces left now of the railway itself, which originally carried timber and coal from the Artikutza basin to the port of Pasaia. This stretch of the walk affords good views through the trees across the Artikutza basin to the hills beyond. A sign indicates some old **millstones** to the right (ERROTARRIAK/MUELAS; **2h35min**) and, further along to the right, a signposted promontory forms a magnificent **natural balcony** overlooking the the entire basin (BALKOI NATURAL/BALCON NATURAL; **2h50min**). The Erroiarri Waterfall can be heard far below, but is not visible from here. Now the path remains level and eventually rejoins the **road** (**3h20min**), just before the point where we originally entered the forest at the start of the walk. Turn right along the road to return to **Eskas** (**3h30min**).

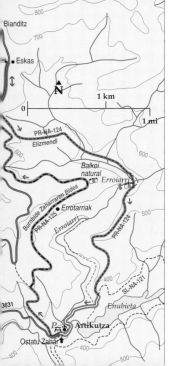

Walk 7: AIAKO HARRIAK (PEÑAS DE AIA) CIRCUIT: ARITXULEGI • DOMIKO IRRIGATION CHANNEL • CASTILLO DEL INGLES • ELURRETXE • ARITXULEGI

See also photograph page 17
Distance: 12km/7.5mi; 4h30min
Grade: moderate, with an overall ascent of 250m. This walk does not involve any major climbs, but there is a fairly steep zigzag ascent through the forest on the return section of the GR121 to Aritxulegi. Well-waymarked; from Aritxulegi to Elurretxe on PRGI-20 (yellow and white), returning on the GR121 Gipuzkoa circuit (red and white).
Equipment: See page 55

Access: 🚗 Follow Car tour 2 on the Oiartzun-Lesaka GI3420 road. Park beyond the cattle grid, on the gravel road which ascends to the right *immediately before* the tunnel at **Aritxulegi Pass**. 🚌 from Plaza de Gipuzkoa in Donostia-San Sebastián to the main square in **Oiartzun**, from where a taxi can be taken to **Aritxulegi Pass** (8km), or alternatively take a taxi from Irún to Elurretxe/Castillo del Inglés, from where you can pick up the route.

Aiako Harriak (Peñas de Aia) is one of the most climbed mountain ridges in the Basque Country, and rightly so. Walking the whole ridge is exhilarating, but reaching the two highest peaks of Txurrumurru and Erroilbide involves some serious scrambling and is not for vertigo-sufferers. The classic route from Elurretxe is described in *Landscapes of the Pyrenees*. The walk described here is a complete circuit of the mountain at between 400m and 500m (the three summits are just over 800m), offering the chance to explore a curious irrigation channel, some beautiful forest and excellent close-up views of the near-vertical south face.

Start the walk at **Aritxulegi Pass** (439m), which marks the border of the provinces of Gipuzkoa and Nafarroa. Walk up the gravel road just before the tunnel to a small **picnic area** (🌲*P*; **5min**) which affords great views back towards the sea and over the surrounding hills. Turn left over the **tunnel** and then right, across the **cattle grid** (**10min**), onto the start of the PRGI-20 path, waymarked in yellow and white. (The path zigzagging up the mountain straight ahead is the shortest route to Erroilbide, the highest of the three peaks of **Aiako Harriak** at 832m.)
Our PR path descends, passes through another **cattle grid**, and reaches the **Bar/Restaurante Aialde**, which has a nice terrace and views over the valley and the

San Antón Reservoir (**30min**). Turn right to rejoin the road and sharp left onto the path marking the start of the **Canal Domiko**. The path by this irrigation channel is narrow in places, so watch your step. This is a beautiful meandering walk through the forest, with tantalizing glimpses down towards the **Endara Valley** and an impressive rocky outcrop, the **Risco de San Antón**, on the other side. Leave the irrigation channel when you reach a signpost indicating ELURRETXE to the left (**1h25min**). The path zigzags up to a small clearing in this mostly oak and beech forest, with a solitary **picnic table**, making a pleasant rest stop (🌲; **1h50min**). Proceed along the forest path, following the waymarking, and just before approaching the

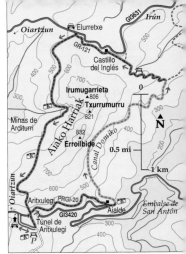

Oiartzun-Irún road, turn left onto an initially unmarked path (**2h**) which runs parallel to the road and then joins the GR121 (red, white and yellow). After descending past two clearings, the path crosses an **old bridge** (**2h15min**) and reaches the remains of a house in the forest, overlooked by several large twisted beech trees. This is the **Castillo del Inglés** (the Englishman's Castle; **2h20min**), the former residence of an English engineer who owned the mining concessions in the area and who in the early 1900s would organize lavish parties here for the wealthy families of Irún. Continue to follow the GR121 up through the forest to the parking area of **Elurretxe** (525m; **2h30min**), the main departure point for the ascent of Aiako Harriak.

To begin the return route, follow the path beside the **fence**, signposted 'ARITXULEGI'. The path hugs the immense granite rock face of the three peaks of Aiako Harriak very closely, and at this height is below the tree line. An **outcrop** (**3h05min**) provides fine open views of the valley of the **Arditurri Mines** below, and beyond them, towards the coast. Soon after, the path crosses a **stream** (**3h15min**) with the peak of **Txurrumurru** towering directly above. This makes another very pleasant shady rest stop. From here it's a fairly steep climb up through the forest, with increasingly clear views towards Donostia-San Sebastián. You emerge above the trees and round the grassy end of the ridge. Another signpost (**4h10min**) points the way on to ARITXULEGI, which soon comes into view as we begin the fairly steep descent down to the junction with the PRGI-20 (**4h25min**) and **Aritxulegi Pass** (**4h30min**).

Rounding Aiako Harriak (top) and the Canal Domiko (bottom)

Walk 8: ETXALAR • SARRIKO ERREKA • BAGOLEKO BORDA • AIZKOLEGI • AZKUA • ETXALAR

Photographs pages 9, 19, 20
Distance: 15.5km/9.6mi; 6h
Grade: moderate-strenuous, with overall ascents of 750m. This fairly long circuit involves a gradual ascent to the highest point, Aizkolegi, and then a short, steep ascent of Azkua. The descent from the ridge back towards Etxalar is also fairly abrupt. Only the final

descent from Azkua is waymarked, but paths are generally very clear.
Equipment: see page 55
Access: 🚗 Follow Car tour 2 to **Etxalar** and park in the centre of the village. 🚌 Donostia-San Sebastián/Elizondo buses stop at **Ventas de Etxalar** on the main road, from where it is a 4km walk into **Etxalar** itself.

This little-trodden route starts from the beautiful village of Etxalar and offers the chance to explore some of the most extensive beech forests in the region. There follows an exhilarating ridge walk just above the tree-line, with great views of the Baztán region and an ascent of Aizkolegi, the highest point of the Señorío de Bertiz Gardens, with its abandoned wooden 'palace' on the summit.

Start out in **Etxalar** (100m): turn right outside the **church**, taking the ZUGARRAMURDI ROAD which

forks to the left. You pass an explanatory board showing walking routes in the area and

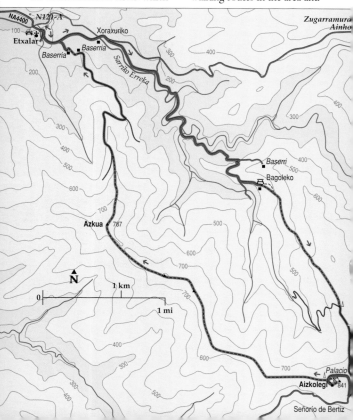

follow signs out of the village towards ARTAKO BIDEA. Cross the stream (**Sarriko Erreka**), head uphill and take the first right turn after **Xoraxuriko** *borda* — a lane signposted CASA RURAL/LANDA ETXEA (**15min**). The lane follows this pretty valley into the forest and is a fairly flat 4km walk. At the first main junction (**1h15min**) proceed straight on towards BAGOLEKO BORDA. Then take the next road, steeply uphill and across a cattle grid, to reach attractive **Bagoleko** *borda* (390m; **1h40min**), perched on the hillside. This, and a couple of other *casas rurales* in the valley, are available for holiday rentals.

Go through the **gate** to the left of the house, beside a picnic table, and turn right immediately along a path which initially follows a **fence** and soon enters the beech forest (**1h50min**), climbing steadily. As the path starts to level out, the ridge along which we return to Etxalar is clearly visible on the opposite side of the valley. Then we re-enter a particularly beautiful section of forest. After a **stile** (**2h05min**) the path converges with a forest track beside a **cairn** (**2h10min**). Take note of this cairn if you will be returning along the same route, as the track heading the other way comes to a dead end deep in the forest! Turn left from the cairn and proceed along the forest track, which contours until reaching a **gravel road** (**2h40min**). Here we turn sharp right up the hill, to an abandoned caretaker's house just below our first summit. Go up the steps to the left, to reach the grassy summit of **Aizkolegi** (841m; **2h55min**), with its observation board and the curious remains of the old wooden *palacio* 'palace' designed by a local Basque who made his millions in America and returned to invest his fortune in

creating the **Gardens of Señorío de Bertiz** (see Car tour 2 on page 19), of which this marks the highest point. The views from the top extend well towards the Pyrenees on a clear day.

Return back down the road and, just before the first bend, look for a **small cairn** in the grass (**3h10min**) that marks the start of a clear path to the left. Follow this as it winds through the forest. Climb over a **stile** (**3h25min**), to emerge on the open ridge, and follow the fence downhill and then up again to the left to the next **grassy summit** (**3h45min**). Still keeping the tree line just to your right, proceed onto the following **summit** (**4h05min**), topped by a clump of rocks. A fairly sharp descent and even steeper ascent brings us to the top of **Azkua** (784m; **4h40min**), with its large concrete summit marker. Below to the right is the valley we followed up to Aizkolegi.

Go straight ahead along this flat summit to the first **wooden pole**, with orange and black markings (**4h45min**; it was visible from the summit) and descend steeply down the mountain spur, with Etxalar directly in front of you. This section is perfectly waymarked with further poles. Turn right on reaching the first track (**5h10min**), then take the next left, signposted to ETXALAR. Follow this track down through the woods until you reach a *baserri* (**5h40min**). Take the path beside it, which passes another, very old *baserri* (**5h50min**) and joins an asphalted lane. Go through the **gate** and down to the ZUGARRAMURDI ROAD, where you turn left through **Etxalar**, back to the church (**6h**).

Walk 9: GOROSTAPALO • IÑARBEGIKO ERREKA • XORROXIN WATERFALL • DOLMEN DE IÑARBEGI • IÑARBEGI • BARRENETXEA • GOROSTAPALO

Distance: 9.3km/5.8mi; 3h20min
Grade: fairly easy, with only a gentle climb of 260m and a stream to cross with the aid of some stepping stones. The route as far as Xorroxín Waterfall makes a nice short excursion with children. The path to the waterfall is waymarked in green and white, and most of the circuit around the Iñarbegi Valley in yellow and white.
Equipment: see page 55
Access: 🚌 Follow Car tour 2 to **Erratzu** and cross over the river bridge beside the church, following the lane signposted GOROSTAPALO. Reach the village of **Gorostapalo** after 1.7 km and park in the main square near the large Dolarea *baserri*. 🚐 bus from Donostia-San Sebastián or Iruña-Pamplona to **Elizondo**, then taxi to **Erratzu** and walk to **Gorostapalo** (allow an extra 20min each way).

T his is a very pleasant, easy circuit starting from the picturesque village of Gorostapalo with its wood-beamed houses, typical of the Baztán region of Nafarroa, and the nearby beautiful Xorroxín Waterfall, deep inside a mainly oak forest. The rest of the walk involves a pleasant hike along the right bank of the Iñarbegi Stream to the valley head, mostly in the forest, and a return route along the hillside on the opposite bank offering open views of the surrounding mountains and pastureland dotted with farmhouses.

Xorroxín Waterfall

Start the walk at the pretty square of **Gorostapalo**: retrace your steps back to the entrance to the village and turn right down the cobbled lane beside the small chapel of **Nuestra Señora la Dolorosa**. Descend to the **Iñarbegiko Erreka** and cross the **stone bridge** (**10min**), then turn right along a track. Soon turn right again along a green and white waymarked path signposted to XORROXIN, now having entered the forest. A further path to the right re-crosses the **stream** (**20min**), from where we continue parallel to the stream until reaching some **stepping stones** (**25min**). Be prepared to get slightly wet here if the stream is quite high, although it's otherwise an easy ford. Continue along the opposite bank to reach the **Xorroxín Waterfall** (**30min**), taking the time to cool off and enjoy this idyllic spot in the forest. Return to the stepping stones and take the path to the right which crosses in front of another, **smaller waterfall**. On reaching the remains of an **old stone wall** to the right (**35min**), take a fairly narrow path which doubles back, initially beside this wall, parallel to the stream and above Xorroxín. When you see a *borda* to the left just above the trees, make straight for it but, before reaching it, turn right on the main path along the **Iñarbegi Valley**, waymarked in yellow and white (**40min**). The path and waymarking are clear and the walk is now a gentle climb through a picturesque part of this mostly oak forest. To the left are meadows on the flanks of **Mt Autza**, which marks the border with France, and several *bordas* (some occupied, some not) are passed along the route. Emerging just above the forest, head right along the asphalt road (**1h20min**) which leads to the scattered *baserri* along the valley. Just off the road, to the left, is the

Dolmen de Iñarbegi (**1h30min**), a good vantage point for views of the valley. Return to the road, fork right, downhill, and then fork right again towards ERRATZU on the waymarked PR4 (**1h45min**). Take the trail straight ahead at the first bend (the main track which veers to the left is private and leads to the **Iñarbegi** farmhouses. Cross the **Iñarbegiko Erreka** (**1h55min**) and proceed up the hill on the opposite bank. The trail initially climbs somewhat and then levels out once on the hillside, with the stream all the time below to the right.

Just before **Barrenetxea** *baserri* (**2h25min**), the trail turns to the left, away from the valley, and takes a fairly meandering, level route back towards Erratzu and Gorostapalo, both of which are now visible ahead. At the next main fork (**2h55min**), take the path down to the right. Where it becomes enclosed by **fences** on both sides (**3h10min**), *leave* the yellow and white waymarked path (which runs straight ahead around the hillside towards Erratzu). Instead, turn right, to descend back to **Gorostapalo** (**3h20min**).

Walk 10: AURTITZ • EMBALSE DE MENDAUR • BUZTIZ LEPOA • MENDAUR • BUZTIZ LEPOA • EMBALSE DE MENDAUR • AURTITZ

Distance: 13.4km/8.3mi; 4h25min

Grade: strenuous, with an ascent of 930m (the final summit ascent is quite steep). Very well way-marked in yellow and white from Aurtitz to Buztiz Lepoa (part of the PR NA104); the ascent from this pass to the summit, and the short descent (200m) from the Mendioder ridge to the reservoir are not waymarked, but are easily followed nonetheless.

Equipment: see page 55

Access: 🚗 Follow Car tour 2 to **Aurtitz**, turning right to enter this small village at the second signpost (when coming from Ituren). Park the car anywhere in or near the entrance to the village. (It is also possible to drive the 5km from Aurtitz to the **Embalse de Mendaur** along a somewhat potholed track, thus reducing the walk to about 2h return. There is a nice picnic site at the far end of the reservoir(🅿️P). 🚌 from Iruña-Pamplona to **Aurtitz** (request stop), involving a change of bus in **Leitza**; otherwise more frequent buses from Iruña-Pamplona and Donostia-San Sebastián to Doneztebe/Santesteban, 6km away, then taxi.

M endaur is the most prominent peak in the Baztán Valley, and this route is the classic one to the summit, via the small reservoir bearing the same name. The summit itself is topped by a small chapel dating back to the 17th century, and the whole route from Aurtitz is extremely varied and picturesque.

Start out from the entrance to **Aurtitz** (200m), by a small square: turn left along a cobbled street running parallel to the main road, then go right at the signpost for MENDAUR. Just beyond the last house in the village (**5min**), turn left along a path, following the waymarking (the lane/track straight ahead at this point also leads to the reservoir). Ascending, you briefly join a track leading to an old *baserri* (**20min**), then turn right again on a second path. This climbs to another track, where you turn left and continue, contouring, until you reach a large **cairn** (**35min**), where you can rejoin the ascent path: take the right-hand fork, signposted MENDAUR. The path follows a stream, crosses a small concrete **bridge** (**50min**), and rises gradually through a particularly pretty section of beech forest, remaining fairly close to the stream. Eventually you rejoin the

Steps to the Mendaur summit

track which has risen from Aurtitz to the **Embalse de Mendaur** (**1h15min**).

Turn left to walk around this small reservoir, with the summit of Mendaur directly above it, to a shady **picnic site** on the far side (**1h25min**; ⌐P). Cross the stream and turn left at the next *borda* (**1h30min**), to climb steeply up the hillside. Once above the tree line, veer left, away from the summit of Mendaur, following the main path towards a large **menhir-like boundary stone** marking the pass (**Buztiz Lepoa**; 935m; **1h50min**).

But before reaching the stone, take the path which zigzags uphill to the right. This brings you to the start of the **60 stone steps** (**2h10min**) leading to the chapel on the summit of **Mendaur** (1131m; **2h15min**). This chapel, the **Ermita de la Trinidad**, dates back to 1692, although it was largely restored in 1963. From the cross behind it, there are wonderful views over the entire Baztán region, with the villages of Aurtitz and Ituren looking a seriously long way directly below!

Descend the same way to **Buztiz Lepoa** (**2h35min**), from where we take a different, scenic route back to the reservoir. Follow the path which continues straight ahead, cut into the hillside of the neighbouring mountain, **Mendioder** (1074m). Continue on this path until it joins the **ridge** (**2h55min**), from where there are excellent views down to the Arantxa Valley on the far side. It is possible to continue west along the top of the ridge to the next mountain, Ekaitza (1047m), in about 30 minutes from this point, but we descend the first spur just after reaching the ridge — taking a clear path directly down to the picnic site by the **Embalse de Mendaur** (**3h15min**).

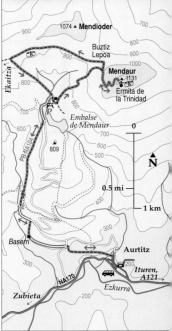

Menhir-like boundary stone marking the pass, Buztiz Lepoa

From here retrace your steps around the reservoir, to where you can rejoin the **path** (**3h20min**) back down through the forest to **Aurtitz** (**4h25min**).

Walk 11: BILBAO • SAN ADRIÁN • LARRASKITU • ARNOTEGI • CRUZ DE ARTABE • PAGASARRI • BIBERDI • GANEKAGORTA • KRUTZIAGA • FUENTE DE AITZIZKETA • BIBERDI • PAGASARRI • BILBAO

Distance: 19.5km/12mi; 6h15min (from Plaza Zabalburu in Bilbao itself, but see also under 'Access')

Grade: The outward walk is basically up … all the way. The full route is a long one, starting as it does practically at sea level and reaching 1000m at the summit of Ganekagorta. For a mountain so close to the city centre, way-marking frankly leaves a lot to be desired, but by following the instructions below there should be no problem, and during high season there are plenty of walkers about to point you in the right direction. The ridge walk approaching and beyond the summit should not be attempted if the top is covered in cloud, otherwise the walk presents no difficulties.

Equipment: see page 55

Access: ⚍ From Plaza Zabalburu in Bilbao's city centre, follow the red sign indicating SAN ADRIAN and, at the first roundabout up the hill (before the motorway), go straight ahead along **Avenida San Adrián** through the suburb of the same name. Cross the motorway bridge, take first right turn and then the first left (beside the Iberdrola electricity substation). Then take the middle fork of three lanes, via **Larraskitu** and **San Justo**. The motorable road ends just before a gate at **Collado de Arnotegi** (4km from Bilbao). Driving here reduces the walking time by 2h. 🚐 No 76 city bus from Plaza Moyua to **San Adrián**. Get off by the **Iberdrola substation** (1.5km from Bilbao); this reduces the walking time by 1h.

Ganekagorta is the only mountain reaching 1000m within the *comarca* of Bilbao. In fact, its real height is 998m, but a 2m-high summit marker has been built to enable it to attain mythical status among locals! The full, albeit long walk from the city centre is recommended to put things in their true perspective, providing an extraordinary contrast between the concrete jungle of the Basque Country's largest city and the surprisingly wild, green mountainous area immediately to the south — the high point of which is a superb ridge walk to the summit and distant views of the whole Bilbao conurbation to the north and mountains in every other direction.

Start the walk from Plaza Zabalburu in **Bilbao**: walk up **Calle Juan de Garay** and go straight ahead at the main **roundabout** along **Avenida San Adrián**. Cross the motorway bridge and take first right turn. Then (**25min**) take the first left (beside the **Iberdrola electricity substation**, just past the No 76 bus stop) along **Larraskitubidea**, keeping the substation to your left.

Next, fork right up the pedestrianised lane, to reach the first houses of **Larraskitu** (**30min**). Turn right along the road and, after the first bend, head up a steep lane

(**Camino Pagasarri**) to the left. This takes you back to the road, just before Bar Athletic (**40min**). You have now gained considerable height above the city, and the views already extend well out towards the Bilbao estuary. There are some surprisingly rustic *baserri*

here, despite their being so close to the city centre. Follow the road until you reach a fork by a couple of houses, with a small bar to the left, at **Collado de Arnotegi** (300m; **55min**). This is the place to leave the car if you are driving to the trailhead.

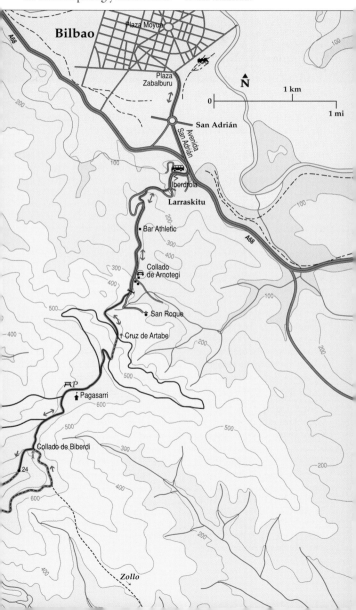

View from the summit of Ganekagorta

Take the right-hand fork, then fork right again (left leads to the church of San Roque, visible on the opposite hillside). Pass through a **gate** (**1h**) and join the start of a forest track, closed to traffic. From here it's a steep walk uphill to **Artabeko Bidegurutzea/ Cruz de Artabe** (**1h15min**). Take the signposted CAMINO VIEJO straight ahead, turn right on rejoining the track (**1h35min**) and ascend to the meadowland and limestone rocks of **Pagasarri** (691m 🗐P), where there is a fine shady picnic site and a **refuge** to the left (www.pagasarri.com for opening times). The city feels a long way away from here!

The Ganekagorta ridge is now visible to the right. Follow the track downhill, taking the left fork by the *agroturismo* sign, and forking left again at the signpost for GANEKAGORTA. You reach a large **electricity pylon** and **concrete marker** at the bottom of the ridge, at **Collado Biberdi** (**2h**). Take the very steep forest track straight ahead which zigzags up the mountain to a **grassy spur** and **marker 24** (**2h15min**). From here a clear path ascends to the ridge and beyond, to the summit marker of **Ganekagorta** (998m; **3h**). Cattle and goats normally

graze on and around the summit, and vultures are also frequently sighted.

Descend just to the right of the ridge, to the next **col**, where there is another white marker (**3h10min**), then take the track which descends to the left. Turn off on the first small path to the left (**3h20min**), which leads to a clearing on the fern-covered hillside. Pinpoint the col below to the left, and look for white markers which guide you fairly steeply down and around the mountain to the **Collado de Krutziaga** (690m; **3h45min**). At the highest point of the col, look for a **large cairn**, from where you take the path to the right (vaguely waymarked in blue). This contours round the sheer south face of Ganekagorta at a height of about 700m.

The **Altzizketa Spring** (**3h55min**) provides the chance to refill water bottles, and from here the next stretch of path completes your circuit of the mountain. Turn left at a signposted **junction** of paths (right leads to the nearest village, Zollo), back to **Collado Biberdi** (**4h35min**). Now retrace your steps via **Pagasarri** (**4h55min**) to **Bilbao** city centre (**6h15min**).

Walk 12: SANTUARIO DE URKIOLA • URKIOLAGIRRE • FUENTE DE POL-POL • PAGOZELAI • ANBOTO • PAGOZELAI • ASUNTZE • SANTUARIO DE URKIOLA

Distance: 10.7km/6.6mi; 4h05min
Grade: The walk is fairly easy as far as Collado de Pagozelai, but then involves an extremely steep ascent of 300m to the ridge just below the summit of Anboto. The final metres to the summit itself are very exposed and demand a head for heights. Detailed instructions are given in the couple of spots where there might be confusion as to the correct path. A shorter, easy alternative is to ascend to Urkiolagirre, descend to the Pagozelai col and return along

the track to Urkiola (about 2h). Total ascent for the main walk: about 600m
Equipment: see page 55
Access: 🚗 Follow Car tour 3 to the motorway exit for **Durango**, and then turn right on the BI623 to **Urkiola Parke Naturala** (13km). Park at Urkiola close to the Bar/Restaurante Bazkarra; if this car park is full, there is another parking area to the left above the *santuario*. 🚌 buses between Durango and Vitoria-Gasteiz stop at **Urkiola**.

A nboto, while not being Bizkaia's highest, is without doubt its most striking and renowned mountain. Since it is the highest point of the spectacular Duranguesado Massif, climbing it gives one the sensation of being in a mountain range the equal of the High Pyrenees or the Picos de Europa. The route described here is the classic one from the Urkiola Sanctuary, entirely within the Urkiola Parke Naturala (nature reserve).

Start the walk at **Urkiola** (700m). First visit the signposted Centro de Información e Interpretación, for maps and details of many walks in the area. Then head up the road opposite the Bar/Restaurante Bizkarra, past the **Basílica de San Antonio** (more commonly called the **Santuario de Urkiola** and one of the most important pilgrimage sites for Basques). It is surrounded by a large and extremely popular picnic

area (🚗P). Just before the **gate** marking the end of the public road (**5min**), turn left up through the woods, following the signpost indicating URKIOLAMENDI and ANBOTO. Cross the **stile** and head up across the meadow, to a small area of **pine forest** (**15min**), then follow the path through the middle of this wood. You emerge on a hillside from where there are superb views to the left, to the lower limestone peaks of the

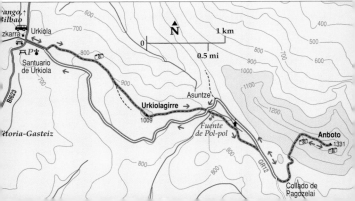

Top: Anboto's summit ridge; below: the Sanctuary of Urkiola at the start of the walk

Duranguesado Massif. Where the main path veers to the right (**25min**), continue straight ahead, following the ridge to the orientation board and summit marker of **Urkiolagirre** (1009m; **35min**). From here there are superb views towards the rest of the Duranguesado chain, with the abrupt face of Anboto rising at the far end.

Descend the spur beyond Urkiolagirre, crossing a stile and reaching a track. You could turn right here, back to Urkiola (a shorter version of the walk). The main walk now descends to the stream and makes for the onomatopoeically named

Fuente de Pol-Pol (**55min**), a large natural spring enclosed by a wooden fence. Follow the path on the right-hand side of the stream until you reach the remains of a peculiar **brick structure** (**1h**), originally used for washing minerals mined in the area. From here ascend past a **refuge**, to rejoin the track crossed earlier. Follow this (it is the route of the GR12) to **Collado de Pagozelai** (**1h15min**).

Turn left at the col, following the signpost to ANBOTO, and start climbing very steeply up through rock and beech woods. The going is tough, but the route is splendidly waymarked in red. There are usually many goats and sheep grazing on the slopes of Anboto, and you will doubtless encounter some sheltering under the trees on hot summer days.

When you reach the main **ridge** (**1h40min**), you will have your first glimpse down to the villages of the Atxondo Valley, 1000m below. Follow the ridge to the right; initially the way is quite safe and not too exposed. You will come to a **marker** (**1h45min**) just below the summit, from where the views back along the ridge are superb. This may be as far as many will wish to climb: the last stretch, to the summit, involves a steep scramble up the exposed south face. While this is not as abrupt as the vertical north face, it *is* somewhat intimidating. If you do reach the summit of **Anboto** (1331m; **1h55min**), you will enjoy a 360° panorama.

From the top retrace your steps to the **Collado de Pagozelai** (**2h45min**) and turn right, returning along the GR12 track to a signpost at the pass of **Asuntze** (890m; **3h**). Turn left, following signs to URKIOLAMENDI along the main track, back to the entrance gate and **Urkiola** (**4h05min**).

Walk 13: LEZIKA • CUEVA DE SANTIMAMIÑE • VALLE DE OMA • OMA • BOLUNZULO • FERRERIA DE OLAKOERROTA • BOSQUE PINTADO • LEZIKA

Distance: 7.4km/4.6mi; 2h40min

Grade: this is quite an easy circuit, with just a short, steepish ascent of 200m from the village of Oma up through the Bosque Pintado (Painted Forest). There is no waymarking, but by following the instructions below there should be no difficulties.

Equipment: see page 55; good trainers are fine for this walk.

Access: 🚗 Follow Car tour 3 to **Kortezubi** and turn left along the road signposted *CUEVA DE SANTI-MAMIÑE* and *BOSQUE PINTADO*. Park beside or just beyond the **Lezika** bar/restaurant (a 2.5km

detour from the main road). 🚌 the Bilbao/Lekeitio bus passes through **Kortezubi**; alight at the crossroads and walk or hitch the additional 2.5km.

NB: Guided tours of the **Santimamiñe Cave** leave at 10.00, 11.15, 12.30, 16.30, 18.00 Mon-Fri only. There is a maximum of 15 people per tour — on a first come, first served basis. The main chamber, which contains the best paintings, is now closed to the public, although a visit to the rest of the cave is still highly recommended.

The beautiful Oma Valley is a wonderful retreat from the pace of modern life, highlights being the unspoilt village of Oma itself with its traditional *baserri*, the unique 'painted forest' — the work of local artist Agustín Ibarrola — and the Santimamiñe Cave, containing the best-preserved cave paintings in the Basque Country.

Start out at the **Lezika** bar/restaurant: walk to the end of the road beyond the main car park. From here, 308 steps take you up via the **Ermita (chapel) de Santimamiñe** and a pretty **picnic site** (⊞P), through forest and limestone, to the entrance to the **Santimamiñe Cave (10min)**. This is a magical place, tucked inside **Mt Erenozar** and home to

the Basque Country's finest cave paintings.
After your visit, descend back past the *ermita,* noting the bust of Joxe Miel Barandiaran, the renowned Basque anthropologist who discovered the cave at the beginning of the 20th century. Back at **Lezika (20min)**, follow the lane directly opposite, down into the **Oma Valley**. On reaching

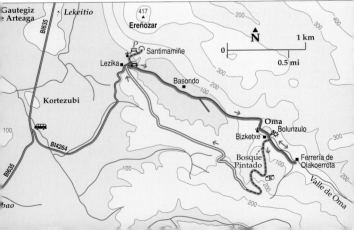

Bosque Pintado (left) and the artist's garden (above)

the valley floor, you pass **Basondo** *baserri* to the left (**30min**). At a signpost for IBARROLA OMA, fork left uphill (**35min**).

This lane passes through a **holm oak grove** and then descends to the picture-postcard village of **Oma**, with its traditional stone *baserri* and a small chapel to the right at the entrance to the village (**50min**). Corn and kiwi fruit plantations line the road as you walk through this village.

Opposite **Bizketxe** *baserri*, cross a small **stone footbridge** over the stream, then follow a narrow path downstream. From here the garden of the artist Ibarrola, containing some of his works, is visible on the opposite bank, before you reach the remains of an old **watermill** in the forest. Just after this point, the stream disappears underground into a huge moss-covered hollow known

as **Bolunzulo** (**1h**). Return to the road (**1h10min**) and turn left, to head past the village and see the remains of an old forge, the **Ferrería de Olakoerrota**, to the left (**1h20min**).

Then retrace your steps to the village but, just before Bizketxe, turn left along a narrow path beside a small stream bordering the grounds of this *baserri*. Go through a gate and cross a stile, continuing up quite steeply into the forest. At the next junction of paths, keep straight ahead on the main path, until you reach the first painted trees of the **Bosque Pintado** (**1h40min**).

From here, the main path zigzags up through this forest of pines — their trunks painted in all manner of strange designs — local artist Ibarrola's unique visual creation. You ascend to a clearing (**1h55min**) from where the views extend back down to the Oma Valley. Continue on the main path, climbing steeply past more painted trees, to leave the Bosque Pintado on a gravel road (**2h10min**). Turn right and follow this road through a eucalyptus wood, to return to the starting point at **Lezika** (**2h40min**).

Walk 14: PAGOMAKURRE • ATXULAR ATE • ITXINA • SUPELEGOR CAVE • LEXARDI • ARRABAKO ATE • ARRABA • PAGOMAKURRE

Distance: 10km/6.2mi; 3h55min

Grade: moderate, with a fairly short, step ascent from the forest to Atxular Ate, the entrance to Itxina. Itxina is a labyrinth of rocks and forest and should not be entered if there is a danger of mist, as it is very easy to get lost, although the route up to Atxular Ate would still be feasible. Waymarking leaves quite a bit to be desired from Pagomakurre through the forest, but more important is the path through Itxina itself, and this *is* quite clearly waymarked in red from Atxular Ate to Arrabako Ate. Detailed instructions are given below in the couple of spots where there might be confusion as to the correct path. A shorter alternative is an out-and-back walk to the

Supelegor Cave (about 6.5km/ 2h30min) — a wiser option on potentially less clear days. Total ascent for the main walk: 340m

Equipment: see page 55

Access: 🚍 Follow Car tour 4 to Artea and continue 2km on the BI3530 to Areatza. Turn right at the square, opposite the church, following signs to GORBEIA PARKE NATURALA. After 2km turn left (4km) towards PAGOMAKURRE. When you reach the **Larreder Atsedelekua picnic site** (9km ⛱P) continue for a further 2km along the gravel road, to the large **Pagomakurre picnic area** (11km ⛱P) and park close to the Bar/Restaurante Pagomakurre. 🚌 Bilbao-Zeanuri buses stop at **Areatza**, from where you can take a taxi to **Pagomakurre** (9km).

Itxina is one of the most fascinating landscapes in the Basque Country and is a truly magical place. It is a karst fortress on the north side of Gorbeia Parke Naturala, Bizkaia's largest nature reserve. Access to this world of strange limestone rock formations, dense forest and the location of the huge mythical cave of Supelegor is via a 'window' in the rock face known as Atxular Ate or Ojo de Atxular — 'Atxular's Eye'. The high meadows of Arraba and views towards Gorbeia — Bizkaia's highest mountain — complete this magnificent circuit.

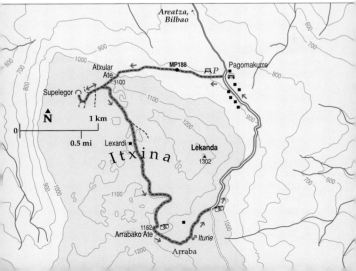

Start the walk from the **Bar/ Restaurante Pagomakurre** (860m), where *bocadillos* and meals are available all year round. Look for the wooden signpost pointing to ATXULAR ATE and SUPELEGOR; follow the path through this beautiful picnic site and enter the **forest** (**5min**). Continue along the main path, looking out for sporadic yellow, blue and red way-marking. Various paths diverge, but run more or less parallel to each other, until you reach **boundary stone MP188** (**20min**). Beyond this stone you start to ascend slightly, on a clearer path which emerges above the tree line. Cross a **stile** (**25min**) and proceed straight ahead towards the immense limestone wall of Itxina. When you cross a second **stile** the 'window' of Atxular Ate comes into view. At the base of the rock face (**35min**), look for red waymarking which guides you

Two views from the orientation board (3h15min): back towards Gorbeia, Bizkaia's highest summit (top) and to Lekanda (left)

steeply up to **Atxular Ate** (1100m; **45min**).

From here you enter the fantasy world of **Itxina**; descend to a large hollow and circle round it, to a junction of paths (**55min**). Here an arrow on a rock points to *SUPELEGOR*. Turn right and descend through the beech forest to a clearing, where you should locate a **metal pole** (**1h05min**) and green marking, indicating 'CUEVA' to the right.

Follow this path. Watching out for the green markings, fork left just after another hollow, to enter a natural **passageway** carved out of limestone (**1h10min**). Turn right and right again (**1h15min**), to descend to a clear path which leads to the immense entrance of **Supelegor Cave** (964m; **1h20min**). It is possible to go quite a way inside the cave, and it is a popular refuge for cows and sheep. This is just the 'tip of the iceberg' of an immense cave system, and Supelegor itself is the focal point of many legends in Basque mythology.

Return the same way to the junction of paths near Atxular Ate (**1h45min**) and turn right, following the red waymarking. The path now winds through the middle of Itxina. Take the right

fork (**1h55min**), still following the waymarking, and climb above the forest to **Lexardi** (**2h10min**), a lone *borda*. The path veers to the left up the hillside and reaches a flat area (**2h20min**) from where Gorbeia, topped by its huge tower, is visible. Descend to a **hollow** (**2h35min**), from where a clear path ascends to the right — to **Arrabako Ate** (1162m; **2h50min**), the pass through which we leave Itxina — and a magnificent viewpoint towards Gorbeia.

Descend on a rocky path to a stream and the beautiful **Arraba meadow**. Cross the stream and make for a sheepfold, just before which is a spring ('*Iturie*'; **3h05min**). Veer left and cross the meadow, noting a *borda* to the left, and reach a motorable track. Make just to the right, to an **orientation board** (**3h15min**). From this point there are the most stunning views of the whole eastern side of Gorbeia and back towards Itxina. Proceed along the track, keeping the walls of Itxina roughly parallel to your left. You pass its highest point — the imposing, sheer rock face of **Lekanda** — as you descend via several *bordas* back to **Pagomakurre** (**3h55min**).

Walk 15: LENDOÑO GOITIA • LA PIEDRA DEL COJO • SENDA NEGRA • LA BARRERILLA • FUENTE DE ITURRI-GORRI • TOLOGORRI • LENDOÑO GOITIA

Distance: 8.2 km/5.1mi; 3h
Grade: moderate. The walk involves a fairly steep climb up through forest and a slightly vertiginous walk along the Senda Negra — a narrow, level path cut into the side of the Bedarbide mountain. Waymarking, in yellow and white in the forest, and just yellow once on the open mountain, is not always clear, although clear instructions are given in the text below for those points where you might be in doubt. Overall ascent 590m
Equipment: see page 55
Access: 🚗 Follow Car tour 4 to Orduña town centre and take the road which starts close to the main square signposted to LA ANTIGUA monastery and the villages of BELANDIA/MAROÑO. This road passes the railway station and the monastery. After 3.5km, turn left on the BI4532 to LENDOÑO

GOITIA, passing a dolmen on the left and a small **picnic site** (☂P), from where there are excellent views of Tologorri. Turn left 300m before Lendoño Goitia, by a large wooden sign, 'RUTA DE ITURRIGORRIA/ITURRIGORRIKO BIDEA'. Park about 100m beyond this point, beside the gravel road (6.5km detour from Orduña).
🚌 hourly service from Bilbao Abando station to **Orduña**, from where a taxi may be taken to Lendoño Goitia.
NB: If driving, you can continue a further 8km along the scenic BI3931 from Orduña to a rustic *agroturismo* and bar/restaurant called 'Guzurtegi' in the hamlet of **Maroño**, just above a small reservoir of the same name, one of the few places to eat in the area and a wonderful viewpoint for Tologorri and the whole Sierra Salbada.

T he magnificent twin prows of Tologorri are visible for miles around and form the most prominent peak of the Sierra Salbada — a long plain which drops away abruptly above the Orduña and Aiala valleys, forming a long cliff face

The twin prows of Tologorri

of about 700m in height above the valley floor. This is the best-known and most scenic route up the mountain, following the famous Senda Negra (Black Path), so called because of the colour of the earth on this mountainside.

Start out at the **parking area** near **Lendoño Goitia** (441m). Continue along the stony track, taking the first fork to the right and ignoring other, minor forks, gradually climbing up through a large beech forest. At a three-way fork marked by a small **cairn** (**15min**), go straight ahead on the main (middle) track. The route then veers to the left, away from Tologorri, climbing more steeply. After a sharp bend, ignore the two paths straight on; instead, take the path to the right waymarked in yellow and white (the first waymarking visible so far on the route; **30min**). After a few metres, look for another **cairn**, which marks the way — up a leafy path to the left. After a short, steep climb, *carefully* look for a jagged stone on the right, topped by a small **cairn** (**40min**), to follow a path to the right. This path is *not* immediately obvious; there is also waymarking on a tree here, but it is quite faded.

Many rocks now invade the path, until we reach an especially large rock with a plaque inscribed 'La Piedra del Cojo' (**45min**). *El cojo* (the lame one) was a local character who walked with a limp and would regularly stroll with his friends along this path and stop to rest at this spot.

The path soon emerges on the mountainside at the start of the Senda Negra (**50min**) which is cut into the rock face of **Bedarbide** (1037m). This is a beautiful path, with superb views towards Tologorri and down to the valley below, *but watch your step!* You will be relieved to reach a beech tree overhanging the precipice (**1h10min**), from where the Senda Negra zigzags up to the **Portillo de la Barrerilla** (**1h15min**), the only access point onto the top of this otherwise near-vertical ridge.

Go through the gate *(portillo)* and follow the path immediately to the right. As this levels out, the summit marker on Tologorri is clearly visible. From here it is an easy walk to the **Fuente de Iturrigorri** (Red Spring; **1h20min** — so called because the surrounding rocks are coloured by the high iron content in the water). Refill your water bottle, then carry on up a clear grassy path, over a stile, and on to the summit of **Tologorri** (1066m; **1h35min**).

In clear weather it is possible to continue walking all the way along to the end of the ridge for about an hour, to **Eskutxi** (1180m), the highest point; otherwise return the same way to the parking area near **Lendoño Goitia** (**3h**).

Walk 16: LALASTRA • RIBERA • DESFILADERO DEL RIO PURON • HERRAN • CAMPAS DE SANTA ANA • RIBERA • LALASTRA

Distance: 13.8km/8.6mi; 4h45min

Grade: moderate, with an overall ascent of 350m. Unusually, this walk involves an ascent on the *return* route, so it is important to conserve energy for this. On the plus side, the scenery in the Valderejo Nature Reserve is stunning, and the village of Herrán makes an excellent rest stop before heading back over the steepest section of the walk to Campas de Santa Ana. Waymarking, in yellow throughout the nature reserve, is excellent (except for the area between Campas de Santa Ana and Ribera). This walk can be conveniently extended over a full day, with a lunch stop in Herrán.

Equipment: see page 55

Access: 🚗 Follow Car tour 4 to the 108km-point and turn right on the A2622 for *PARQUE NATURAL DE VALDEREJO/VALDEREJO PARKE NATURALA*. Turn left at **San Millán de San Zadornil** and then right in **San Zadornil** village, to continue to the village of **Lalastra**, the main entry point for the park (a 17km detour on a good road). Park in the large car park just before the village entrance. 🚌 from Vitoria-Gasteiz direct to **Lalastra** on Sat/Sun *only* (Bóveda-bound bus).

The Valderejo Nature Reserve is a veritable paradise for walkers. There are many well-waymarked *sendas* (paths) within the park, details of which are available from the Casa del Parque/Parketxea in Lalastra, which also rents out binoculars for viewing the huge variety of bird life. The outward route described here is the classic one, visiting the abandoned village of Ribera and the beautiful gorge *(desfiladero)* of the Purón River, before ending in the village of Herrán in Burgos province. We return on a little-frequented path over the high meadowland of Santa Ana.

Start out from the car park just before **Lalastra**: walk through this pretty village, which has a large, pleasant picnic site. Pass Valderejo Etxea, a conveniently-located *agroturismo* (tel: 945 353085) which also serves meals, and the church, worth visiting for its restored clock tower. Turn left by the **Casa del Parque/Parketxea** (**5min**), to follow **Senda Purón** towards *RIBERA*. This track affords fine open views over the northern part of the park — pastureland surrounded by a semi-circular cliff face several kilometres long. Just after entering the mostly Scots pine forest, go straight ahead at the first junction of paths (**25min**). You descend to a stream, the

Arroyo Polledo (**40min**), and then follow the **Purón River**, eventually going through a gate (**55min**). Follow the signs into the abandoned village of **Ribera**, and climb up to the old **church**, which still contains some fairly well-preserved frescos (**1h**). Return to the main path and turn right to continue along Senda Purón, past a small **picnic site** (**1h 05min**; 🍴*P*) and across meadowland where there are usually plenty of cows and horses grazing. Pass through a gate, to enter more woodland and the entrance to the **Desfiladero del Río Purón** (**1h25min**). Some steps to the left take you steeply down to the river, to a delightful spot close to a

*Ribera's abandoned church (top)
and a farm building in Lalastra*

couple of small waterfalls.
Return to the main path
(**1h35min**) and continue down
through the gorge to a **footbridge**
at the narrowest point. All too
soon we round a bend and leave
the gorge proper (**1h45min**) —
although the scenery is no less
dramatic, with the cliff on the
opposite side of the river being
one of several prime nesting sites
in the park for Griffon vultures
and other birds of prey. A clearing
just above a **waterfall** (**1h55min**)
is another viewpoint over the
lower gorge. Continue past a
junction with Senda Sta Ana and
through a second narrow gap in
the rocks. You join a motorable
track, pass another riverside **picnic
site** (**2h15min**; *⊼P*) and enter
the pretty village of **Herrán**
(**2h20min**).
Take advantage of this pleasant
rest stop (two small bars serve
food and drinks), then retrace
your steps to the junction with
Senda Sta Ana (**2h45min**) and
turn right to follow this narrow
stony path. It zigzags fairly steeply
up the mountain, with tremen-
dous views back down to the
Purón Gorge and beyond to the
plains and mountains of Burgos.
From **Campas de Santa Ana**
(**3h15min**), a flat meadowland,
follow signs back towards RIBERA
on a well-waymarked path down
through another Scots pine forest.
When you emerge at a meadow
(**3h30min**), locate the church in
Ribera to the northwest and *head
straight downhill across the meadow
towards it* (the waymarking posts
on the this section have been
mostly removed — by cattle!).
Meet a track (**3h40min**) and turn
left, back to **Ribera** (**3h50min**).
From here retrace your steps on
the **Senda Purón** to **Lalastra**
(**4h45min**).

Walk 17: OKINA • RIO AYUDA • BARRANCO DE ARROLA • PLANICIE DE MONTESINOS • SASETA • RIO AYUDA • OKINA

Distance: 11km/6.8mi; 4h
Grade: moderate, with an easy, almost level walk along the Ayuda River, followed by an ascent of 200m up the Barranco de Arrola. The ascent in some cases follows the stream bed itself and can be a little overgrown. Although the Ayuda Valley route is reasonably waymarked in red and white (part of the GR38 Ruta del Vino y del Pescado), waymarking is non-existent on the longer Arrola section. By following the directions in the text, however, there should be no difficulties. For a shorter version, walk as far as Saseta and return the same way (2h30min return).
Equipment: see page 55; trainers

are fine for the shorter return walk along the Ayuda River.
Access: 🚌 From Vitoria-Gasteiz, the easiest way of reaching Okina is to follow signs east out of city to the N104 towards IRUÑA-PAMPLONA and DONOSTIA-SAN SEBASTIAN (the *old* road, *not* the new dual carriageway). Turn right (2km) on A132 towards ESTELLA and then right again on the A2130 (4km) to the village of **Otazu**. Just past this village, take the signposted minor A3104 road towards OKINA. The road ends in the tiny village of **Okina** (17km from Vitoria-Gasteiz). Park in the village. There is no public transport along these roads; you must take a taxi from Vitoria-Gasteiz.

T his walk offers the chance to explore the wild and unspoilt, forested Montaña Alavesa. The main walk, along the Ayuda River between the tiny villages of Okina and Saseta, makes an extremely pleasant excursion from Vitoria-Gasteiz. But with the right footwear, the full walk up the Barranco de Arrola is highly recommended — and less than half an hour's drive from a major city.

Start the walk in **Okina**, but first look around the Romanesque village church. Then take the lane diagonally across the square from the **fountain**, to the left of a map providing information about the GR38. Now in the valley of the **Río Ayuda**, you go through a **gate** (**10min**) and enter a beech forest. The remains of an **old watermill** are visible on the right (**15min**) and, a little further on, to the left, a **refuge** (**20min**) marks the border with the County of Treviño, a curious enclave belonging to the Castillian province of Burgos within the Basque territory of Araba! A small wooden bridge crosses the **Barranco de Arrola** just after this point, and this is the route to take

if you are just doing the shorter out-and-back walk to the village of Saseta.
The main walk turns left just after the refuge, to follow an initially-clear but unmarked path on the left side of the stream. The path crosses it a few times and for much of the way follows the stream bed. Stay as close as possible to the stream itself; after **45min**, there appears to be a path up the hill to the left, but *ignore* this and keep straight on. As the vegetation thickens, make your way over the rocks on both sides of the stream until you reach **a small waterfall beside a yew tree** (**1h05min**), although by this point the stream may already be little more than a tiny trickle.

100

Take the path just before the waterfall; it circles above the falls towards the top of the **escarpment**, then returns to cross the stream about 100m/yds higher up, now above the trees (**1h10min**). The going is now easier and, as you double back towards the edge of the escarpment, look back down the **gorge** you have just ascended, for great views towards the Ayuda

Near Okina

Valley. The path is fairly clear along the top but, as you progress, make for a large solitary **holm oak** directly in front of you (**1h30min**). About 20m to the left of this tree, pick up a **track** which winds its way along the top of the **Planicie de Montesinos**, an uncultivated, fairly windswept plain covered in scrub. Follow this track all the way south, to descend to the Río Ayuda, then continue straight ahead where it joins a path just before the river (**2h10min**). The track crosses a small stream and joins the main valley path (**2h25min**), then comes into **Saseta** (**2h30min**). This village belongs to the County of Treviño. Having once been almost abandoned, some of the old farmhouses are now being restored as permanent homes. There is a small rustic bar with garden (Bar Larrein) to the right as you enter the village, which is open at weekends throughout the year and daily in summer. You can usually get a meal but, in these fairly remote parts, it's best not to rely on this!

Leave the village by the same route and, at the first junction (**2h40min**), fork left (look for the fairly faded red and white sign on a fence post). Go through a **gate** (**2h45min**) — and enter the most beautiful part of the valley. At times the path climbs fairly high above the **Río Ayuda** and at others runs just alongside it. The whole valley is luxuriant with vegetation. There are many little **picnic spots** beside the river, and a particularly nice **rock pool** (**3h**) with crystal-clear water. Further on, near a rock overhang, there is a **waterfall** beside the path (**3h20min**).

Cross the wooden bridge over the **Barranco de Arrola** (**3h40min**) and retrace your outgoing route back to **Okina** (**4h**).

Walk 18: KRIPAN • CALZADA ROMANA • ALTO DEL AVELLANAL • BONETE DE SAN TIRSO • ERMITA DE SAN TIRSO • NACEDERO DEL KRIPAN • KRIPAN

Distance: 11km/6.8mi; 4h15min
Grade: moderate, with an overall ascent of 650m. A fairly winding ascent up through the forest and onto the ridge all the way to the monolith and cave-chapel of San Tirso. The final 200m/yds of ascent to the summit of San Tirso itself requires care, and there are a couple of sections (especially in the last few metres) that demand a head for heights. The route is initially well signposted from just outside Kripan and then waymarked in white and yellow and/or orange all the way to San Tirso, but the waymarking in the forest is not always clear.
Equipment: see page 55
Access: 🚗 Follow Car tour 5 to **Kripan**. The walk starts from the village square. Or, to reduce total walking time by 1h, drive to the source of the Kripan River: on Car tour 5, take the lane to the left by the km74 Vitoria road marker (just before Kripan), and park at the picnic site (2km from main road). Pick up the main walk just after the 25min-point (see map). 🚌 The Elvillar bus from Logroño (La Rioja) runs via **Kripan**.

This is a beautiful walk up through forest to the top of a ridge and the huge rock monolith of San Tirso. Just below the summit is a cave-chapel. This is one of the more easily accessible and spectacular parts of the Sierra de Toloño-Cantabria. You then descend to a lovely shady *merendero* (picnic site) in a gall-oak grove, where you come upon the *nacedero* (source) of the Kripan River. At both the start and end, you follow the remnants of an old Roman road.

Start the walk in **Kripan**. From the square, take **Calle Matilla**, heading north towards the mountain ridge overlooking the village. Cross the main road and continue along an unsurfaced road signposted to EL NACEDERO and BERNEDO. From here the route is marked in white and yellow. At a **water tank** (10min) take the left fork. This section partially follows an old *calzada romana* (Roman road), although the original paving is not very obvious. On reaching a road (**25min**), head right, uphill, still following the *calzada* and the same waymarking (signpost: VUELTA A LOS PUERTOS). This is a shady stretch, and the old paving stones of the *calzada* are in better condition here.
Take the next left fork (**35min**),

San Tirso, with view towards La Población

onto a wider track which winds up through the forest. As the track veers left, note an orange arrow on the left, indicating the path which will be your return route. Just after this, ignore the track joining from the right (**40min**); keep straight on. Fifteen minutes later, *turn sharp right* to continue on the main route (faint waymarking). Reaching a signposted **crossroads** (**1h**), head left for PUERTO DEL ELVILLAR. (The route to the right, signposted to Bernedo, is the original route of the *calzada romana* over the sierra.) The path now ascends through a beautiful section of beech forest. As you rise to the ridge, you have tantalizing glimpses through the trees of the Bernedo Valley on the north side of the mountain. You soon come to two signposted **crossroads** (**1h20min**) a short distance apart; first turn left towards PUERTO KRIPAN and then, about 100m further on, at **Alto del Avellanal**, turn right for SAN TIRSO. Now firmly on the ridge, but still among the trees, this beautiful path meanders gradually upwards until the huge **Bonete de San Tirso** (1280m; **1h40min**) rock monolith comes into view directly ahead. From here the views are spectacular — towards the plain of La Rioja to the south and the heavily forested Montaña Alavesa to the north. Continue past the monolith on a clear path to the rock face of Mt Tirso itself, until you reach the cave containing the ruins of the **Ermita de San Tirso** (**1h50min**). A *romería* (religious fiesta) takes place in this cave-chapel every year on 15th May. A very steep path zigzags up behind the cave and onto the exposed ridge above it. This becomes very narrow and vertiginous in places, as it ascends to the top of **San Tirso** (1329 m; (**2h05min**). From here retrace your steps past 40min-point of your outgoing route and, when you reach the orange arrow (**3h15min**), turn right down the narrow path. This plunges down through gall oaks and joins a track (**3h25min**). Turn left and reach the picnic site at the **Nacedero del Kripan** (**3h30min** ⊼*P*), the source of the river. There is a drinking fountain here and plenty of benches in the shade. Walk up through the trees along the grassy track to the right of the picnic area and when you reach the brow of the hill, take the narrow path to the right, to reach the cave of **Ermitaño** (**3h40min**), inside a huge rock overhang. Retrace your steps to the picnic site and continue along the initially gravel, then asphalted road, to the crossroads with the *calzada romana* (**3h50min**). Turn right to retrace your outgoing route to **Kripan** (**4h15min**).

Walk 19: SANTUARIO DE KODES • GENDARMES • LA LLANA • IOAR • LA LLANA • SANTUARIO DE KODES

Distance: 7km/4.4mi; 3h
Grade: fairly strenuous, with a short but steep ascent of just over 600m from the Santuario de Kodes to the summit of Mt Ioar. There are no technically difficult sections on the walk, and the route is well waymarked all the way to the summit.
Equipment: see page 55
Access: 🚐 Follow Car tour 5 to **La Población** and continue for a further 5km. Then turn right at the top of the pass, on the minor road towards *AGUILAR DE CODES* and *PAMPLONA*. From **Aguilar** (2.5km) follow signs to the *SANTUARIO DE NUESTRA SRA DE KODES*, 3km beyond the village of **Torralba del Río** (a detour of 11km detour from the car tour route). Park the car in the car park just above and to the left of the **Santuario de Nuestra Sra de Kodes** and guest house.

This route ascends Mt Ioar, the second-highest peak in the Sierra de Toloño-Cantabria/Sierra de Kodes range, on the border of Araba and Nafarroa. The climb is via the fantastic vertical rock formations known as the 'Gendarmes'. The going is pretty steep, but the superb scenery more than compensates for the effort, and the views from the summit are the best for miles around.

Start the walk from the car park to the left of the **Santuario de Nuestra Sra de Kodes** (800m): take the red- and white-marked path to the right of the explanatory board, close to a small picnic site (🚐P) above the sanctuary. At the first *borda*, take the right-hand fork; this heads fairly steeply up through a quite dense, mixed forest, with many young oaks.

View from the Collado de la Llana down past the Gendarmes to the village of Torralba del Río

Just before emerging from the forest (**30min**), take the path to the left, marked by the large pile of stones and with the same way-marking. The immense vertical rock pinnacles of the **Gendarmes**, guarding the entrance to the pass, now tower directly in front of you. The path becomes rocky and zigzags up the mountain, slightly to the right of these pinnacles. Look out for vultures circling around the Gendarmes — as well as higher up, around the summit.

Beyond the pinnacles you reach the bottom of a **scree slope** (**50min**). While there is a path to the summit directly up this scree, it is extremely steep. So keep to the main path, which climbs less steeply to the right and soon reaches the **Collado de la Llana** (1200m; **1h05min**), a flat grassy pass marked by a cairn. Take the path to the left* from the pass, marked in red; this ascends the grassy hillside and offers increasingly open views across the heather-covered **moorland** towards the long, comb-like ridge of Costalera at the far end of the Sierra de Kodes behind you. The large TV mast on the summit of Ioar now comes into view and, as you climb, you enter an attractive **beech forest** (**1h20min**).

Emerging by the **TV mast** (**1h30min**), turn left for about 10-15 metres, above the mast, for the best views back down towards the sanctuary and the striking rock formations known as the **Dos Hermanas** (Two Sisters), at the base of the ridge directly below. Then continue to the summit of **Ioar** (1418m; **1h35min**). Walk

*From the pass you could take a detour to right, following the *blue* markers. This leads along the main ridge to the summit of La Plana (1331m) in 20 minutes.

View up to the Gendarmes guarding the pass

on just past the summit, to a cairn with a curious **mini-sculpture of a tree**, from where you will have the best views of the Sierra de Toloño-Cantabria and La Población to the west and towards the Izki Nature Reserve to the northwest.

Return the same way to the **Collado de la Llana** (**2h**) and from there back down the mountain, to your starting point at the **Santuario de Nuestra Sra de Kodes** (**3h**).

Walk 20: ANTOÑANA • BUJANDA PATH • KORRES GORGE • KORRES VILLAGE • EL AGIN PATH • SOILA • ANTOÑANA

Distance: 9.5km/5.9mi; 3h45min
Grade: moderate-strenuous. The walk ascends gradually through forest, along the Korres Gorge and then on to the ridge of Mt Soila. But the descent from the ridge is a bit tricky: at first it is somewhat exposed and vertiginous, then the stretch through the upper forest is steep and can be slippery after rain. This route is almost entirely within the Izki Nature Reserve and is splendidly waymarked in yellow throughout with a series of numbered footpaths (*sendas*). Overall

ascent/descent: 400m
Equipment: see page 55
Access: 🚍 Follow Car tour 5 to **Kanpezu** and turn left on the main A132 towards VITORIA-GASTEIZ. The walk starts 5km along this road, at the beautiful medieval 12th-century walled village of **Antoñana**, founded by King Sancho the Great of Navarre. Park either beside the main road or by the fountain at the entrance to the village. 🚐 11 from Vitoria-Gasteiz (Estella and/or Contrasta bus); alight on the main road in **Antoñana**.

T his is an interesting, very varied circuit around one of the most beautiful parts of the Izki Nature Reserve, a recently-created *parque natural* in the relatively little-known area of the Montaña Alavesa. Much of the walk traverses dense forest with yew, maple and ash, among many other species. The gorge and village of Korres are especially attractive, and the return along the Soila ridge spectacular.

Start out at **Antoñana** (607m): cross the main road by the bus stop and follow signs for KORRES along a track beyond the disused **railway station**. The track soon enters the forest. Turn left at the first main, signposted junction (**15min**), following **Senda Antoñana No 15**. Turn left again at the next junction (**25min**); this path will link up with the main path, the Senda Bujanda. Ahead you have fine views of the steepest face of Mt Soila (we will ascend the mountain from the *other* side). The path descends to the beginning of the **Korres Gorge** and joins the main route, the **Senda Bujanda No 1**, beside an **irrigation channel** (**40min**). Turn right and proceed up this heavily-forested gorge, with the river barely visible below to the left. Divert 50m to the left, to the small **Aranbeltz Reservoir** (**50min**).

As you reach the far end of the gorge (**1h05min**), turn right* up the lane into the pretty old village of **Korres** (**1h10min**). Wander up through the narrow streets of the village, stopping to visit the 16th-century church of San Esteban, to the wooden kiosk above the bridge, which serves as the **information centre** for the Izki Nature Reserve (**1h15min**). A good walking map of the park and other information is available here. Turn right outside the kiosk and then left onto **Senda el Agin No 14.**

Follow the yellow waymarking, ascending gradually through wood and scrubland until the ground becomes rockier (**1h45min**) and the path zigzags up to the ridge,

*A left turn, downhill, here leads in five minutes to an excellent picnic site (🍴P) just outside the gorge.

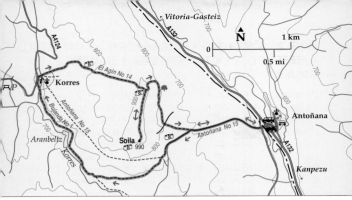

Arriving in Korres (top) and the ridge descent from Soila on the Senda el Agin

with increasingly open views towards the Sierra de Toloño-Cantabria. The **ridge top (2h)** itself appears somewhat abruptly after a relatively gentle ascent, and affords great views down to Antoñana. Follow the signpost to the right along the ridge to the summit of **Soila** (990m; **2h15min**), from where the Korres Gorge is now visible to the right. Vultures are commonplace here. Take the time to descend slightly, to a curious **natural window** in the sheer rock face (accessed via a hollow just below the summit). Retrace your steps along the ridge to the **signpost (2h40min)** and continue along the narrow Senda el Agin, cut into the rock. The path turns sharp right **(2h45min)** and plunges into the forest below the cliffs (a rope helps on some of the trickier passages). You descend past ash and maple trees and reach a giant, ancient **yew** tree beside an explanatory board **(3h05min)**. The yew is now a protected species in the Basque Country.

A series of steps takes us further down through this beautiful forest, then we cross a forest track with fencing on both sides **(3h25min)**. Keeping straight on, descend to the junction first passed at the 15minute-point **(3h30min)**. Turn left, back to **Antoñana (3h45min)**.

Walk 21: BAQUEDANO • RIO UREDERRA • WATERFALLS • NACEDERO DEL UREDERRA • BALCON DE PILATOS • BAQUEDANO

Distance: 8km/5mi; 3h30min
Grade: easy. The walk follows the Urederra River, with a slight ascent (under 100m) towards the end and a further short steep ascent (100m) to the water catchment area near the source. Most of the walk is within a nature reserve and, although the path is not waymarked beyond the village of Baquedano, it is clear throughout. While the walk may be easily completed in the time shown, it's worth spending much longer, to

enjoy the river and forest.
Equipment: see page 55; trainers are fine for this walk.
Access: 🚍 Follow Car tour 5 to the junction with the NA718 and turn right in the direction of ESTELLA. Pass through **Zudaire** and after 2.5km turn left onto the NA7187 towards BAQUEDANO. After a further 2km you reach **Baquedano**; there is a car park just to the left (a detour of 5.5km from the car tour route).
NB: There is *no* public transport.

The Urederra River is one of the most beautiful spots in the Sierra de Urbasa, with its turquoise pools and series of waterfalls, and most of this walk provides a wonderful shady escape from the heat in high summer. The route ends just before the river's source *(nacedero)* — directly below the awesome cliff face of the Balcón de Pilatos. There are few more idyllic river walks in the Basque Country.

Start out from the **car park** at **Baquedano**: walk up through the village, following the sign 'NACEDERO DEL RIO UREDERRA'. The main track to the source starts behind and to the right of the large *frontón* (pelota court) in the village square (**5min**). Go past the **Bar/Restaurante Urederra**, which has a map of the Urbasa area on the wall and, once out of the village, take the first fork to the left (by a group of **holm oak trees; 15min**). Passing through a **green gate** (**20min**), fork left again, downhill towards the river. A **second gate** (**25min**) marks the end of the track and the start of the path through the nature reserve and into the forest proper. Steps take you down to the left (**40min**), to the **Río Urederra** and the first of the **waterfalls** with its turquoise pool. This, and the other most visited sections of the river, are roped off, although it is easy enough to climb down to the

water's edge. Reclimb the steps and continue along the path closest to the river, mostly in the shade of a beech forest.
You come to an equally stunning second **waterfall** and pool (**50min**), then cross a **stile** (**1h05min**). The path now climbs gradually, gaining height above the river. Take the path to the left which crosses a small **stone bridge** (**1h20min**). This leads to a clearing in the forest, beyond which a fenced **viewpoint** provides the first close-up look of the cliff face ahead. Cross a **wooden bridge** (**1h35min**) and continue rising through dense forest and over rock. You pass another **waterfall**, then reach the **main footbridge** (**2h**) at the head of the valley, directly above the largest **waterfall**.
Follow the path on the other side, with the river now to your right, until you reach a flat area, still in the forest. Beyond is another

108

Emerald pool on the path to the source of the Urederra

waterfall and a view up to a rocky promontory reminiscent of a natural diving board: this is jutting out from the top of the **Balcón de Pilatos** — several hundred metres directly above you (see Car tour 5).

Returning to the flat area just above the river, follow a steep narrow path, zigzagging further uphill — to a small **water catchment** (**2h15min**), close to the **Nacedero del Urederra** and almost at the top of the tree line. This is as high as it is practical to follow the course of the river up the cliff face without actually rock-climbing. This last section is well worth the extra effort, for the great views to the Balcón de Pilatos, but watch your step when descending.

Descend the same way back through the forest until you reach the **stile** passed earlier (**2h50min**). If you wish to spend more time by the river, retrace your outgoing route back to Baquedano.

The main walk varies the return by forking left here, following a path beside a fence. This path returns directly through the forest to the **green gate** (**3h15min**), through **Banquedano** (**3h25min**) and back to the **car park** (**3h30min**).

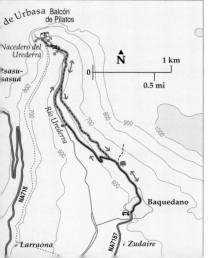

109

Walk 22: CASA FORESTAL DE ARALAR (GUARDETXE) • PAGOMARI • ERRENAGA • IGARATZA • TRIKUARRIKO LEPOA • IRUMUGARRIETA • TRIKUARRIKO LEPOA • UNAGAKO PUTZUA • URDANGOENE • ALBIA • GUARDETXE

Distance: 14.2km/8.8mi; 4h45min

Grade: moderate, with a gradual gain in height of 400m over several kilometres. The most important point to note, however, is that once above the forest, it is very easy to get lost on the high pastureland of the Sierra de Aralar when the mist comes down. The full circuit described here should only be attempted on clear days. A shorter, easier alternative is the walk to Igaratza and back along the forest road (3h return).

Waymarking is fairly reasonable, and detailed instructions are given below in the couple of spots where there might be confusion as to the correct path.

Equipment: see page 55

Access: 🚗 Follow Car tour 5 to the **Guardetxe/Casa Forestal de Aralar**. Leave the car in the large car park to the left. 🚌 Buses running between Donostia-San Sebastián and Iruña-Pamplona stop at Lekunberri, 12km from the start of the walk. There taxis are available.

T his is a varied circuit through the beech forests, high pastureland and karst landscape of the central part of the Sierra de Aralar, an area which is also renowned for its many neolithic remains. The walk culminates with an ascent of

Returning along the GR12, near Trikuarriko Lepoa

Irumugarrieta, the highest mountain in the range — quite easily reached without major exertion, since the starting point of the walk is at 1000m.

Start the walk from the **Guardetxe** (1035m), the rustic forest guard's house (open throughout the year, serving meals, *bocadillos* and drinks). Walk to the far end of the car park and go through the green gate. Walk along the unsurfaced forest road until an arrow indicates a path to the right (**5min**). Follow this path, roughly parallel to the road, admiring the forest of mainly beech trees.

On reaching a walled enclosure beside the road, you can peer down into **Beingo Leizea** (**15min**), a deep limestone chasm. Rejoin the road a little further on (**20min**) and follow it past **Pagomari** (**40min**), a flat area which provides the first open

views of the karst landscape and mountains of the sierra. Continue climbing gradually through the forest, to emerge on the open mountain just beyond **Mandarrate** (**1h**), a small pass where the road narrows as it cuts its way through the limestone.

Continue along the road which now veers to the right. At the highest point in the road, **Errenaga** (1220m; **1h15min**), climb up to the fence to the left, to look down on the **refuge and chapel of Igaratza**. From this point practically the whole Aralar range can be seen.

Just after the **MP90 marker**, leave the road (which descends to Igaratza), by forking right. You head across pastureland, directly

111

On the summit of Irumugarrieta

climbed in Walk 4 and shown on page 56.

Descend the same way to the small stone marker at **Trikuarriko Lepoa** (**2h40min**), then turn left to follow a clear path which is partially waymarked in red and white. Pass the **Obioneta dolmen** (**2h55min**) and come to **Unagako Putzua**, a waterhole usually well-frequented by the many horses grazing on this pastureland (**3h10min**). Remain on the main path, first descending slightly to the left and then climbing to **Urdangoene** (**3h35min**), the pass beyond the end of the **Txameni** ridge. At the pass, fork right, away from the GR12, and descend a valley, following a stream which takes its source just below the pass. After descending a bit, follow the red waymarking into the forest, passing a small *borda* to the right (**3h55min**) and later a **headstone** with a *lauburu* (Basque cross; **4h05min**).

From here follow faint yellow and white marking, although the path is fairly obvious. At a clearing with a faint junction of paths (**4h15min**), turn right, passing another *borda* to the left (**4h20min**). The path now becomes wider and stonier, passes a third *borda* and joins the road. Turn right, past the **Albia dolmen** beside the road on the right (**4h 30min**), and follow the road back to the **Guardetxe** (**4h45min**).

towards the limestone mass of Irumagarrieta. The red and white markings of the GR12 guide the way, although these are not immediately visible when leaving the road. On reaching a small stone marking a pass (**Trikuarriko Lepoa; 1h30min**), turn left to the remains of the **Trikuharri dolmen** (**1h35min**).

From here follow the clear red waymarking over the limestone, veering to the left at the **MP83 marker** (**1h50min**), to come up onto the main ridge. Once up on the ridge, cross the **fence** (**2h**) and continue to the summit of **Irumugarrieta** (1431m; **2h10min**), from where the views to the valley 1000m below and along the whole ridge are awesome. The pointed peak to the west, at the far end of the range, is Txindoki, the summit

Walk 23: MONASTERIO DE LEIRE • CAÑADA REAL DE LOS RONCALESES • LA CERRADA • CASTELLAR • EL RALLAR • ARANGOITI • EL RALLAR • MONOLITO DE LEIRE • MONASTERIO DE LEIRE

See map opposite

Distance: 9.2km/5.7mi; 4h45min

Grade: moderate-strenuous, with an overall ascent of 700m. This walk starts off with a steady ascent following the GR13, which is not always well waymarked. Once on the ridge — and in particular between the two passes of La Cerrada and El Rallar — waymarking is rudimentary at best (a mixture of cairns, occasional paint daubs, and small ribbons tied on trees). The path is quite overgrown and rocky in places, so the going is fairly slow. On the plus side, by keeping going more or less in a straight line just below

the top of the ridge and using the large TV mast on the summit of Arangoiti as a landmark, there should be no problem. The short-cut descent from El Portillo del Rallar back to the monastery is steep, but safe and not exposed.

Equipment: see page 55

Access: 🚗 Follow Car tour 6 to just beyond the village of **Yesa**, and turn right on the NA2113 for 'MONASTERIO DE LEYRE' (4km from Yesa). Park the beside the monastery. 🚌 The Iruña-Pamplona-Uztarroz bus stops at **Yesa**, from where it is a walk of just over 4km up to the **Monasterio de Leire**.

The Leire Monastery, perched high above the Yesa Reservoir, provides the dramatic starting point for this walk, which follows one of the old drovers' roads from the Pyrenean valleys to the dry southern region of Nafarroa. An interesting section along a ridge culminates in an ascent of the highest mountain in this part of central Nafarroa, with awesome views towards the Yesa Reservoir area, the Aragón River and the canyon of the Foz de Arbaiun.

Admire the ornately carved 12th-century Romanesque portico and the Gothic/Romanesque nave and vaults at the **Monasterio de Leire** (771m). Then **start the walk**: return to the **car park** and look for the GR13 red and white waymarking, which starts just beside an information board about the **Cañada Real de los Roncaleses** — one of the most historic of the old Pyrenean drovers' roads. Pass the remains of a derelict **shepherd's hut** (**5min**) and follow a gully marking the course of a long-dried-up river bed. The waymarking is a bit haphazard from here on, but by following it up through the forest, you can't really get lost. Mostly holm oaks grow in the gully, although these

give way to beech and pine as you climb. The going gets increasingly steep and, after crossing a forest track for the third time, the trail (still following the gully) veers to the right. **Cairns** mark this spot (**30min**): note that the cairn to the left, just above the narrow path, marks the end of our return route, when we descend from the ridge near the end of the walk. The GR13 narrows beyond the gully, with a particularly attractive cobbled stretch, before emerging on the ridge at the **Portillo de la Cerrada** (1230m; **1h25min**), a high pass marked by a rickety old signpost. From here there are great views down to the monastery and towards the rock face of Castellar, topped by a large cross

113

Arangoiti, with its huge TV mast,
is visible to the right.
Return to the ridge path. Some
clambering over rocks is required,
and the path is quite overgrown in
places. The odd faded red paint
spot, and small ribbons tied to tree
branches help somewhat, but
basically keep contouring just to
the right of the ridge top, until
you reach a small clearing with a
cairn, marking **El Portillo del
Rallar** (**2h15min**). *Take note of
this cairn for the return journey, as it
marks the start of the direct descent to
the monastery.*
Proceed straight ahead on the
path, still in the forest, before
emerging temporarily above the
tree line at a point from where the
canyon of the **Foz de Arbaiun**
(see Car tour 6) can be seen to the
right (**2h25min**). From here the
path is clearer and better marked
by cairns, as it runs along the top
of the ridge with increasingly open
views towards the Yesa Reservoir.
On reaching a **barbed-wire fence**,
cross a stile and emerge at a third
pass (**2h45min**). You then pass
an **electricity transformer station**
and ascend the final ridge. Here
you join the private surfaced road
coming in from the north and
follow it to the summit of **Arangoiti** (1335m; **3h05min**).
Return the same way to the
Portillo del Rallar (**3h55min**),
and turn right by the cairn. The
path descends steeply through the
forest, to emerge by a
promontory (**4h05min**) directly
above the monastery and close to
the **Monolito de Leire**, a large
rock monolith about a third the
way down from the rock top.
Descending steeply all the way,
rejoin the GR13 and turn right
(**4h30min**). Follow the **gully**
mentioned above, back to the
Monasterio de Leire (**4h45min**).

— this is our next landfall.
Here we *leave* the GR13 by
making for some **boulders** to the
left of the pass. Tiny cairns mark
our ongoing path between these
boulders, but they are usually no
more than just a couple of stones,
so keep your eyes peeled. Climbing up through the forest, keep a
clump of large rocks to your right
and, when you emerge at the
highest point, divert left (as indi-
cated by a couple of arrows carved
into the rock) to **El Castellar**
(1281m; **1h40min**). This
promontory offers the best views
towards Yesa and beyond —

Walk 24: CASAS DE IRATI • CAMINO VIEJO A KOIXTA • EMBALSE DE KOIXTA • CAMINO VIEJO A LAS CASAS DE IRATI • MIRADOR DE AKERRERIA • NUESTRA SEÑORA DE LAS NIEVES • CASAS DE IRATI

Distance: 10.2km/6.3mi; 3h25min

Grade: quite easy, with an overall ascent of 300m. The walk, largely through forest, follows the course of the Urtxuria River to the small Koixta Reservoir. The path is quite narrow for the first 1km above the river, so take care until you have crossed the first stream, after which the valley widens out somewhat. The circuit combines two well-waymarked routes among many around the Forest of Irati, in this case the SL.NA69 and SL.NA60A. In the main car park by the Irati River there is a kiosk staffed by park wardens (open daily 15/6-15/9; weekends only 1/4-15/6 and 15/9-30/11). Here you can get maps and other information about the many walks in the area. Even though this walk is relatively short, a whole day is recommended to enjoy the surroundings and to picnic by the river.

Equipment: see page 55

Access: 🚗 Follow Car tour 6 to Ochagavía and turn left on the NA2012, signposted to IRATI. This road crosses the long ridge of Mt Abodi. At the top (Tapla Pass; 1400m) there are maps detailing two more short, interesting walks along the ridge. The road then descends into the forest and ends by the **Irati River**, where there is also an excellent picnic site (🏕P). Park in the main car park by the river (a 23km detour from Ochagavía). 🚌 daily from Iruña-Pamplona as far as **Ochagavía**, from where an option could be to follow the GR11 from the village northwards to the **Casas de Irati** (8h return). Otherwise there is no public transport.

T he Selva de Irati is one of the largest forests of beech and fir in Europe, extending over both sides of the Pyrenees. This circuit is perhaps the best in the area in terms of variety: not only is most of the walk inside the forest, but the route follows a scenic path beside the Urtxuria River to the small Koixta Reservoir nestling below the Mt Ori (2000m). We also visit the superb natural rock balcony of Akerrería above the forest and the interesting area around the Casas de Irati.

View down to the road to Casas de Irati from Tapla Pass

Selva de Irati

Start out from the **car park** by the **Irati River**: walk back up the road for about 300m, to the start of the **Camino Viejo a Koixta**. This old trail initially climbs steeply to the right, up into the forest. At the point were the trail re-crosses the road (**10min**), the GR11 forks off to the right, but we follow the green and white waymarking of the SL.NA69 to the *left*. Soon after this path starts to narrow above the river (**25min**), *leave* the main path (which appears to carry straight on). Turn sharp left, to zigzag down closer to the river. The path is at its narrowest here, but this is the most beautiful section of river and forest on the walk.

After crossing three tiny streams, the path emerges on a track (**1h20min**) which we follow to the small **Embalse de Koixta** (**1h35min**). **Mt Ori** (2021m) looms directly above the reservoir, beyond the forest.

116

To start the return walk, cross the **dam** and turn left along a track, the **Camino Viejo a las Casas de Irati**. This initially runs parallel to the river, but then veers to the right, crosses a stream and ends (**1h45min**). From here take a path climbing quite steeply up through the forest, to emerge in a clearing (**2h15min**), with fine views towards the long, flat Abodi ridge. Cross some pastureland before re-entering the forest, and divert left to the **Mirador de Akerrería/Akerriako Begiratokia** (**2h25min**), a rock perched high above the river and a superb natural balcony over the forest.

Return to the main path, which descends very steeply to a forest track (**2h50min**), which is quite muddy in places. Follow the SL.NA60A signpost directing you back onto a small path (**3h05min**) which forms part of a short **nature trail**, along which the main types of tree in the forest are labelled. The nature trail rises to the small hilltop chapel of **Nuestra Señora de las Nieves** (**3h15min**). From here descend past the ruins of the **Casas de Irati**, originally used as a fort during the Napoleonic wars and subsequently as a forest guard's house. The circuit is complete when we reach the **car park** by the **Irati River** (**3h25min**).

Walk 25: FABRICA DE ARMAS DE ORBAITZETA • SOROLUZE • ARNOSTEGI • URKULU • SOROLUZE • AZPEGI • FABRICA DE ARMAS DE ORBAITZETA

Distance: 11.8km/7.3mi; 3h45min

Grade: moderate, with an ascent of 600m. A fairly gradual climb up to the Col d'Arnostegi is followed by a short but steep ascent from there to the summit of Urkuku. Waymarking is excellent throughout, partially following the Trans-Pyrenean GR11, although there is a possibility of getting lost in cloudy weather in the somewhat confusing karst landscape around the summit.

Equipment: see page 55

Access: 🚗 Follow Car tour 6 to **Aribe** and, after crossing the river, turn right on the NA2080,

following signs to ORBAITZETA. Continue through **Orbaitzeta** (5km) and, at the next crossroads (8km; where a right turn leads in 1km to the Mendilatz refuge (open Mar-Dec; beds, bunks and restaurant; www. mendilatz.com) continue straight ahead to the signposted **Fábrica de Armas de Orbaitzeta** (10km). It is also possible to drive beyond this point on an unsurfaced road to **Azpegiko Aterbea**, a small refuge, reducing the walk by 4km/ 1h15min. 🚌 Iruña-Pamplona to **Orbaitzeta** village, from where it is necessary to walk or hitch the last 5km.

The Roman tower on the top of Urkulu, perched right on the French-Spanish border, provides a magnificent viewpoint over the Western Pyrenees. The shortest way to the summit is from the French side, from the Col d'Arnostegi, a route described in *Landscapes of the Pyrenees*. This walk starts from the Spanish side, from the curious remains of an old weapons factory used during the 18th-century Carlist wars, and also incorporates an interesting circuit of several important megalithic sites on and around the Col d'Azpegi.

Park the car just beyond the remains of the old **Fábrica de Armas de Orbaitzeta** (830m), at a small ramshackle collection of houses with an old church, the latter now being used to store farm machinery. It's worth looking around the eerie ruins of the old weapons factory, which are now quite overgrown, with the river flowing through the middle. The factory was originally built mainly to supply cannons to the army of Carlos III of Spain (Carlos V of Navarre) in the 18th century.

Then **start the walk:** head along the unsurfaced road to the left of the **church**, and fork right beyond the last house, following the GR11 towards AZPEGI. This is a

motorable road and in fact continues right over the border into France, although most people leave their cars at the *fábrica*. Take the next right fork (**15min**) and, following the course of the stream, come to **Azpegiko Aterbea** (**40min**), a small emergency refuge with a spring and information boards about walks in the area.

Just beyond here, leave the road, forking left to follow the path signposted RUTA MEGALITICA DE AZPEGI, waymarked by small yellow dolmens. The scant remains of the first couple of **dolmens** are soon visible on the right, close to the stream. At the next signpost (just before a *borda*; **50min**), turn left towards SOROLUZE. This is a

117

Summit of Urkulu

to enter a narrow pass and arrive at **Soroluze** (**1h15min**). A well-preserved dolmen is just to the left and another beside a tree a few metres further on.

Ignore the signpost to the right to Urkuku (this will be our return route); instead keep straight ahead, enjoying the open views towards Askozibar and the valley below and more or less contouring along the hillside to the **Col d'Arnostegi** (1260m; **1h30min**). The mountain road which climbs up from St Jean-Pied-de-Port/ Donibane Garazi ends here; there is a large animal drinking trough and the **205 marker** stone, on the French/ Spanish border.

From here a clear a path ascends steeply, waymarked in yellow, to a flat area of karst rocks (**1h50min**) just to the right of the summit; make your way over these to climb up the steps to the summit of **Urkulu** (1419m; **1h55min**), crowned by the impressive remains of an old **Roman watch tower**.

For the return, at first retrace your steps down towards the flat area, but then carry straight on through the karst landscape, taking care to follow the yellow waymarking until the path becomes clear as you descend the grassy hillside to **Soroluze** (**2h20min**). Turn left to retrace your steps, forking left at the signpost first passed at the 50min-point. Pass the *borda* (**2h40min**) and join a track which circles the *borda* and meets the unsurfaced road slightly higher up the valley.

Turn left to the **Col d'Azpegi** (1060m; **2h50min**), just to the right of which is a well-preserved **cromlech**. From here return along the same road, past **Azpegiko Aterbea**, to the **Fábrica de Armas de Orbaitzeta** (**3h45min**).

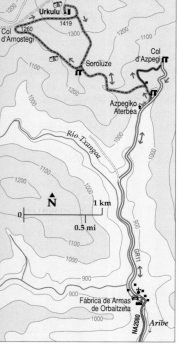

pretty ascent up through mainly beech forest, following the course of the stream. The route then rises on the open fern-covered hillside,

Walk 26: OLHETTE • LARRUNGO ERREKA • TROIS VEAUX • LARRUN • ZIZKUITZ • LARRUN TXIKI • VENTA YASOLA • DESKARGAHANDIKO LEPOA • OLHETTE

See also photograph page 61
Distance: 11.8km/7.3mi; 4h30min
Grade: strenuous. The walk involves an overall ascent of 835m from Olhette, initially a steady climb along the GR10 to the Col des Veaux (563m) and then a fairly steep ascent to the summit at 900m. The descent is more gradual, except for a steep section from the ridge down to Venta Yasola.
Equipment: see page 55

Access: 🚗 Follow Car tour 7 on the D4 to **Olhette**. When the road reaches the highest point in the village, opposite a salmon-coloured *fronton*, take the country lane signposted LE CHEMIN DE MONTTUBAITA to the right. This ends after 1km at a large farm-house. Park in the signposted car park to the right, just before the *gîte d'étape*. 🚌 St Jean-de-Luz/ Donibane Lohizun to **Ascain**, then taxi to the start (4km).

L arrun is the last proper mountain in the Pyrenean chain before the Atlantic. The pronounced peak, with its large transmitter and collection of bars/restaurants (photograph page 61) is visible from far away and is one of the region's best known landmarks. Its funicular, which dates back to 1924, makes it easily accessible to day-trippers, and in high season and at weekends the top can get pretty crowded. Nonetheless, this itinerary is a beautiful circuit which follows two very scenic sections of the GR10 and then descends an exhilarating and surprisingly little used ridge.

Start the walk from the **car park** near **Olhette**: walk down the lane opposite the *gîte d'étape* and cross **Larrungo Erreka**, where there is a GR10 sign on a tree pointing to LARRUNE. Go through the gate at the far end of a second parking area, beyond where the initially flat, rocky, waymarked path ascends to the right (**10min**). You soon climb above the forest onto the open hillside — and your first clear view (**20min**) of the whole **Cirque de Larrun**, which we will follow in its entirety on this walk. This section of the GR10 also offers open views back towards the coastal French Basque towns and across to the Spanish side. Keeping to the left above the

119

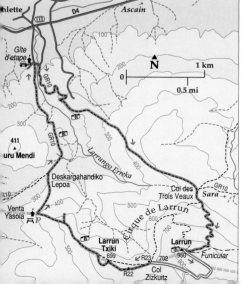

Larrungo Erreka all the way, the wide path ascends to the **Col des Trois Veaux** (563m; **1h25min**), a major junction. The GR10 veers left here, down towards the village of Sara. Our route turns *right* just *before* the col (and the beginnings of a small pine wood), along a well-defined path: follow orange arrows painted on the rocks. Beyond the edge of the wood, the path takes a sharp turn to the right (**1h40min**) and zigzags up the mountainside towards the summit directly above you. There are several short cuts, but the main (less steep) path follows the yellow signs as far as the **funicular tracks** (**2h15min**). From here follow the tracks to the summit of **Larrun** (950m; **2h30min**) with its large transmitter, bars/restaurants and orientation board. Take the time to enjoy the incredible views towards the coast and the Pyrenees and then, to escape the crowds,

walk down the gravel access road which descends fairly steeply on the Spanish side beyond the **Udako Etxea bar** (**2h35min**). Descend to **Col Zizkuitz** (702m; **2h55min**) and continue along the path behind **border stone R23** (*not* waymarked). Keeping a small beech forest to your right, circle the hill, ignoring the path which descends to the right, continuing on to **border stone R22**. From here a short, gentle ascent brings you to the summit of **Larrun Txiki** (Little Larrun; 699m; **3h10min**), topped by a large cairn. A small path is visible below, just beyond the cairn. Descend to join this path (which avoids a scramble down the rock face at the end of the ridge), and rejoin the main ridge path below.

Now an exhilarating ridge walk leads you down to the edge of a **larch forest** (**3h30min**) on the left, from where a five-minute diversion to the right takes you up to another quite impressive rocky outcrop. The path now drops steeply, with the forest to the left, to **Venta Yasola** (**3h50min**; ⊓P), a small refuge with picnic site, where you can buy drinks during high season and most weekends. Follow the yellow arrows on the rocks down to **Deskargahandiko Lepoa** (Col des Contrebandiers; **4h05min**), where the path rejoins the GR10. From here a pleasant, easy descent with more fine views to the Cirque de Larrun on the right, returns us to the **car park** near **Olhette** (**4h30min**).

Larrun, and the tourist train (above)

Walk 27: PAS DE ROLAND • LEGARRE • AMEZKETA • PIC DU MONDARRAIN • HARLEPOA • GARROA • PAS DE ROLAND

Distance: 8.7km/5.4mi; 3h
Grade: moderate, with an overall ascent of 700m. From the Col d'Amezketa to the summit of Mondarrain is a fairly steep climb of 270m, and the descent from the summit to the road directly below is also steep in places. By following the instructions below, a scramble over rocks to the summit and a similar descent from it may be avoided. The upward route is mostly waymarked in yellow, although the return route beyond

the initial descent from the summit is not. The walk should not be attempted if cloud is obscuring the summit area.
Equipment: see page 55
Access: 🚗 Follow Car tour 7 to the **Pas de Roland**. Park by the Hotel/Bar Pas de Roland. 🚂 One train a day stops at **Itxassou** on the Bayonne/St Jean-Pied-de-Port line, from where a taxi is required (3km; for a taxi telephone Larronde Jean Pierre at Itxassou, tel: 0675675260)

M ondarrain, despite its fairly modest height, is one of the most interesting mountains to climb in the French Basque Country, and this circuit offers extraordinary views over this scenic area of hills and gorges. The beautiful summit itself is covered with old, twisted beech trees amidst a chaos of rocks.

Start the walk at the **Pas de Roland** by walking along the road towards ARTZAMENDI — between the pretty Hotel/Bar Pas de Roland (40m) and its refuge. Then, before the *frontón,* take the first right turn, up a lane (look out for the yellow waymarking). Then leave the lane and take the path straight on (**5min**; more yellow waymarks). The rocky summit of Mondarrain soon comes into view towards the left (**15min**) as the path climbs the hillside. Continue straight on at a **crossroads** (**25min**) and then turn left (**35min**), at a sign for MONDAR-RAIN. Go through a **gate** and turn right up another lane. This leads to the **Col de Legarre** (349m; **45min**), where there are a couple of farmhouses.
Turn left along the path sign-posted CIRCUIT DU MONDARRAIN ET DE L'ARTZAMENDI, to circle the smaller **Pic d'Ezcondray** (550m), crossing a **cattle grid** (**55min**). Continue to the small pine wood

on the **Col d'Amezketa** (476m; **1h05min**).
Go around the wood and start the steep climb up the grassy north spur towards the summit; the path is clearly waymarked in yellow. You reach the pre-summit area of twisted **beech trees** and **moss-covered rocks** (**1h25min**). When you come to the large rock face below the summit, *ignore* the yellow arrow pointing to the left (this path involves a somewhat tricky climb); instead, circle to the right of the summit until the waymarking reappears. Now you can take a zigzag path up through the rocks to the summit of **Mondarrain** (749m; **1h40min**), where there is an old stone cross. The views across the valley to transmitter-topped Artzamendi and back towards the Pas de Roland are fantastic.
Before descending, pinpoint your downward route by locating a **farmhouse** just to the left of a lane, about 350m/yds below the

Pas de Roland, with Mondarrain in the background

left of the col. Before reaching this, and once the ground starts to level out, head left around the base of the summit until a path again becomes visible. (There is some blue waymarking, but it is not very clear.) Keep Artzamendi and the valley parallel to your right.

On reaching a couple of large **beech trees** (**2h**), take the path which plunges down the hillside to your right (just after the second tree). At the next fork, head right. When you reach a **fence**, follow it steeply downhill — to the **lane** you identified from the summit (**2h20min**). Turn right along this lane, past **Harlepoa etxea** (**2h25min**), descending round a hairpin bend, and turn left along an unmarked lane beside a small **stone cottage** (**2h35min**) with a delightful rock garden. Beyond the last house at the end

summit looking back towards the Pas de Roland. Then descend on the initially waymarked path directly behind the cross towards the **col** and **pastureland** (**1h50min**) immediately to the south, thus avoiding an extremely steep clamber down the rocky east face. Note the **sheepfold** to the

of this lane (called 'Garroa'; **2h45min**), go through a gate and follow a narrow path which descends the hillside and runs through the **woods**. Back on the Artzamendi road, turn left and pass the *frontón*, to return to the **Pas de Roland** (**3h**).

Walk 28: AROUCHIA • HARPEKO SAINDOA • MARTIKOENA • PEÑAS DE ITSUSI • BEHEREKOETXEA • SUMUSAKO BORDA • BERNATENEA • AROUCHIA

Distance: 11.2km/7mi; 5h
Grade: strenuous, with an ascent of 450m. The ascent on the GR10 between Bidarrai and Ainhoa is steep and fairly exposed in places, although no scrambling is involved. A 15-minute section of path from the GR10 to Martikoena at the beginning of the Peñas de Itsusi is narrow and demands a head for heights, but this may be avoided by going further up the GR10. The rest of the walk is straighforward, although once off the GR10 the paths are not well waymarked. The walk should not be attempted when there is a risk of cloud descending below the Peñas.
Equipment: see page 55
Access: 🚗 Follow Car tour 7 to the **Pas de Roland** and continue towards BIDARRAI. On reaching the valley floor (about 300m past the 101km-point), turn right along the narrow lane up the valley of the **Baztán River**. You initially pass some typically colourful French Basque houses. The gorge offers numerous pleasant picnic sites (🛆P). After 2km, take the lower lane to the right. Some 4km further on you cross a bridge and ascend 1km to the **Arouchia** farmhouse (with green-painted shutters), where the tarmac ends. Park just before the farmhouse, by the GR10 sign to AINHOA.
🚂 There is a train from Bayonne/Baiona to Pont d'Enfer below Bidarrai, but no taxis. It's a 6km walk from the station to the **Arouchia** farmhouse — an option only for very fit walkers.

The somewhat tough climb up to the Peñas de Itsusi is amply rewarded. You visit the unusual cave of Harpeko Saindoa, follow one of the more exciting sections of the GR10 as it passes through the French Basque Country, take a beautiful ridge walk along the entire group of crags making up the Peñas de Itsusi (with the opportunity of seeing vultures at close range), and you return along the wild and unspoilt Aritzakun Valley on the Spanish side of the border. There are many beautiful places to stop once you're up on the ridge, so be sure to allow a full day for this excursion.

Start the walk from the **Arouchia** farmhouse (270m): follow the GR10 sign towards AINHOA, going up **steps** and keeping left (**5min**) alongside a **drystone wall** as the path climbs the hillside. Follow the red and white waymarking to a series of **steps** leading to the cave of **Harpeko Saindoa** (**20min**). This is a place of partly Christian, partly pagan pilgrimage, as evidenced by the bizarre collection of offerings, among them pieces of clothing, dolls and rosaries. The water dripping from the 1.23m-high stalactite just inside the cave to the left is believed to cure skin diseases.

Returning to the GR10, continue up and round the hillside; the path becomes steeper as it enters a **gorge** below the peak of **Zelahiburu** (**45min**), where care is needed in places, as you clamber over rocks. A slight scramble takes you up to a **ledge** (**1h**). This makes a good rest stop, with a view across the valley to the impressive pyramidal peak of

123

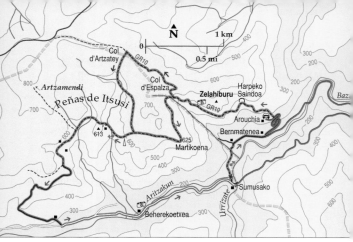

Irubelaskoa in the south. Climbing higher, take the narrow path to the left (**1h10min**) which crosses the stream and hugs the opposite hillside. It is quite narrow and a bit vertiginous in places, but should present no problem to the sure-footed walker. (Alternatively, you can continue steeply up the GR10 to the Col d'Artzatey and from there follow a path around the highest point of the Peñas de Itsusi to rejoin the route on the ridge.)

The **Peñas de Itsusi** begin at the grassy promontory of **Marti-koenea** (625m; **1h25min**). The path now continues upwards and along the top of this wonderful series of spectacular crags high above the Aritzakun Valley. Vultures can usually be spotted perched on the rocks below. When a curious **dog-shaped rock** comes

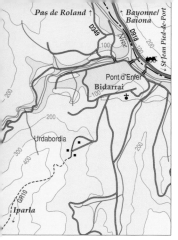

The path has been waymarked in yellow since the dog-shaped rock, but we now *leave* the yellow-waymarked path (which continues towards Mt Artzamendi). Cross a stream and follow a path past a rock marked with a yellow cross (*ignore* the fact that a cross means 'wrong way'). Descend past a still-used **shepherd's hut** (**2h50min**). There is another, lower hut across the field to your left. Take the farm track forking left, to zigzag down towards the valley. Just before the entrance gate to the field of a large white **farmhouse** (**3h30min**), veer right on a path and descend to a gravel road along the **Aritzakun Valley** (**3h35min**). This remote place is actually in Spanish Nafarroa.

Turn left and walk along the road, past a beautiful stone cottage (**Beherekoetxea; 3h55min**), from where there are fantastic views back up to the Peñas de Itsusi. Beyond the old **Sumusako** *borda* (the last house in Nafarroa) you reach a parking area and a bridge over the **Urrizate River**, which forms the border with France (**4h15min**). Retrace your steps about 100m past this house, then take the path to the right. This descends to the **Aritzakun River** (called the Baztán River on the French side) just before the two rivers converge. Cross the rickety old **footbridge** (**4h25min**) and climb a path waymarked in scarlet paint up through a beautiful forest and past a small waterfall. On reaching an old **stable** (**4h40min**), turn right along the farm track to **Bernatenea** farm (**4h50min**) and continue up the lane to the **Arouchia** farmhouse (**5h**).

into view below to the left, descend to it (**1h50min**) and continue to a **waterfall** (**2h05min**) which drops over 200m into the valley below. Cross the stream just above the waterfall, to a derelict **shepherd's hut**, and circle a **dry stone wall**, to reach the next *peña* (613m). Then fork right, away from the valley, to cross another couple of **streams** in an area of pastureland (**2h40min**).

Peñas de Itsusi from the Aritzakun Valley

Walk 29: URCURAY/URKOI • DOMAINE XIXTABERRI • IRAMALDA • COL DE IRAMALDA • URSUIA • IRAMALDA • URCURAY/URKOI

Distance: 11.4km/7mi; 3h30min
Grade: The ascents are fairly gradual, although the final section to the summit is a bit steeper. The only waymarks (yellow) are on the return section below the Col de Iramalda, as you follow the course of a stream.
Equipment: see page 55
Access: 🚌 Follow Car tour 7 to the village of **Urcuray/Urkoi**. Turn left down the lane just before the *boulangerie*, signed 'DOMAINE XIXTABERRI', and take the first left turn, to park in the car park beside the *frontón*. 🚌 St Jean-de-Luz/Donibane Lohizun to Cambo and Hasparren service passes through **Urcuray/Urkoi**.

The large rounded hill of Ursuia, being somewhat north of, and separate from, the main Pyrenean chain, is one of the best viewpoints from which to take in the whole range from a slight distance. This walk makes a very pleasant circuit, ascending via a grassy, fern-covered ridge and returning on a picturesque, shady path which follows the course of a stream from its source below the summit.

Take the time to look around the village church at **Urcuray/Urkoi**, which has a half-timbered house curiously built onto its side! Then **start the walk**: follow the asphalted lane signposted to the *DOMAINE XIXTABERRI*, a farm which offers rural accommodation and farm products in the summer months. Keep to the main lane, always following the green *lauburu* (Basque cross) signs, until you reach the **Domaine Xixta-berri** car park at the end of the lane (**30min**). Keep straight on along the fenced track, to a **col** with a small **farmhouse** and **barn** (**40min**). Turn right by the barn and, on reaching a further junction of paths — where the rounded summit of Ursuia rises to the left across the valley — fork right, steeply uphill, initially with a fence just to your right. (A green arrow on a tree trunk indicates the way, but this arrow is not immediately obvious.)

When the path levels out (**50min**), turn left (immediately after a cattle grid), following the fern-covered

Col de Iramalda and (right) returning alongside the stream

tracks at the col. Turn right beside a small derelict farm building, initially following yellow waymarks. Then take the next left fork (**1h30min**). The motorable track climbs steeply and joins a lane heading towards Ursuia. Turn left, off the lane, on a path which crosses a tiny stream and rises to a **grassy spur**. Follow the spur uphill to the right, parallel to the lane you have just left and, on reaching another **col** (**1h40min**), go straight ahead to the summit of **Ursuia** (678m; **1h55min**), topped by a large cairn. Enjoy the extraordinary views towards the Pyrenees to the south (the mountain directly opposite is Baigura).

Descend the same way to the spur just above where you left the lane (**2h15min**). But instead of returning to the lane, head right, downhill, to a **barn**. Here join another track, waymarked in yellow, and follow it to the left, back to the **Col de Iramalda** (**2h25min**).

Turn right at the col, then take the next right turn, down a track which follows a stream from its source just below the col. When the track crosses the stream (**2h40min**), fork right on a path waymarked in yellow. This continues beside the stream — a delightful return through cool, shady woodland, with the stream descending the valley in a series of small water-falls. Wooden markers indicate names in French and Euskera of the many different trees along the way. You emerge on a lane (**3h15min**) with an information board about the Ursuia area. Turn left here, rejoin your ascent lane, and turn right to return to **Urcuray/Urkoi** (**3h30min**).

Iramalda Ridge (428m) and keeping the Pyrenean peaks to your right (the rocky summit of Mondarrain and the globe-shaped transmitter on Artzamendi are easily distinguished). Go through a **wooden gate** and then two **metal gates**, still on the top of the ridge, before descending to some old farm buildings at the **Col de Iramalda** (395m; **1h15min**). On reaching the first building, go over the **stile**, turn left and pro-ceed across the junction of farm

Walk 30: LOGIBAR • PASSARELLE D'HOLTZARTE • HOLTZARTE FOREST • OLHADÜBI GORGE • OLHADÜBI BRIDGE • PLATEAU D'ARDAKOTXIA • LOGIBAR

Distance: 11km/6.8mi; 4h20min
Grade: strenuous, with an ascent/ descent of 600m. The route to the hanging bridge of Holtzarte is quite steep in places, but a handrail provides assistance on the steepest parts. The path as far as the bridge is well used, and a shorter alternative would be to just go there and back (3.2km/ 1h25min). Following the main

walk, the final descent to Logibar (on the GR10) is extremely taxing on the knees. The walk is waymarked in green and white as far as the Plateau d'Ardakotxia, and from there in red and white (GR10).
Equipment: see page 55
Access: 🚗 Follow Car tour 8 to the car park behind the bar/refuge of **Logibar**. *No public transport.*

The Himalayan-style hanging bridge of Holtzarte, suspended over 200m above the Gorge of Olhadübi, is probably the best-known landmark in Xiberoa and a must for all visitors to the area. This circuit visits the bridge as part of a somewhat longer walk than the usual two-hour return trip, offering the chance to explore the Holtzarte Forest and the upper reaches of the Olhadübi Gorge, with a return descent on the GR10.

Start out from the car park behind **Logibar** (375m): cross the river bridge and turn right to enter the forest and walk alongside the river. The route starts to climb quite steeply over rocks (**15min**) and, on reaching a clearing, the

Holtzarte Gorge and the mountain peaks beyond it come into view (**20min**). Continue along this clear path until you reach the confluence of the **Holtzarte** and **Olhadübi** gorges, a spectacular viewpoint (**40min**),

with the incredible **Passerelle d'Holtzarte** above the latter gorge to the left. When you reach the bridge (580m; **45min**) cross it. Despite its swaying movement, no accident has ever been recorded here! It was originally built in the 1920s as part of a programme of forestry exploration in the area. Once on the far side, take the path zigzagging up through the **Holtzarte Forest**, with tantalizing glimpses through the trees of the Holtzarte Gorge to the right. This path was once part of the GR10, but it is no longer much used, so the red and white markings have faded considerably; still, the path is reasonably clear.

On reaching a wider forest track (780m; **1h10min**), turn left, following the sign to OLHADÜBI along a wide, level path which crosses a stream just below a small **waterfall** (**1h35min**). A little further on, a larger **waterfall** in the main Olhadübi Gorge is visible through the trees (**1h45min**), and we soon reach the small wooden **Olhadübi Bridge** (840m; **1h50min**) at the head of the Olhadübi Gorge.

Cross the bridge, following the sign to ARDAKOTXIA/LOGIBAR along a path which leaves the forest and continues along the hillside with increasingly open views to the gorge. After crossing another stream, the path gently climbs to a flat grassy area (**2h30min**) with stunning views. From here we veer right, up the hillside, to a track. Follow this to the left, to a GR10 signpost at the top of the **Plateau d'Arkatotxia** (980m; **2h50min**), the highest point of the walk. Follow the sign directing you down the track, descending gently towards Logibar and re-entering the forest. Turn sharp left on a waymarked path (**3h20min**) and go over a **stile**, emerging from the forest onto a **grassy spur** (**3h45min**), from where there are fine views down to the Larrau Valley ahead. The final descent, beginning at the bottom of the spur (**4h05min**), is extremely tough going, but steps help over the steepest sections as the path enters the forest again and descends to the car park at **Logibar** (**4h20min**).

Below: Passerelle d'Holtzarte

Walk 31: SANTA GRAZI/STE-ENGRÂCE • PONT DE GAZTELUGAR • GORGES D'EHÜJARRE • GROTTES DE MOLERSE • ERRAITZ • UTZIGAINA • BOIS D'UTZIA • SANTA GRAZI/STE-ENGRÂCE

Distance: 11.6km; 7.2mi; 6h15min

Grade: fairly strenuous, with an ascent/descent of 900m. This is quite a long circuit and can easily be spread over a full day. The path up the gorge involves crossing the stream several times, but for most of the year there is not enough water for you to get wet. There is a short, steep ascent from the Erraitz meadowland up to the

track at the start of the return walk and a noticeable, prolonged descent through the forest back to Santa Grazi. The entire route is excellently waymarked (old green and white waymarks, plus newer yellow markings).

Equipment: see page 55

Access: 🚗 Follow Car tour 8 to the 11th-century Romanesque church in Santa Grazi/Ste-Engrâce. *No public transport.*

T he province of Xiberoa is famous for its immense canyons, and this tour of the Gorges d'Ehüjarre is an incredibly beautiful circuit which follows the bottom of the gorge all the way from the church at Santa Grazi to the high meadowlands of Erraitz. The walk returns along the top of the canyon via Mt Utzigaina, with a descent through the Utzia Forest.

Start the walk from the **church** in **Santa Grazi/Ste-Engrâce**, where there is a map showing the route and a brief description in French

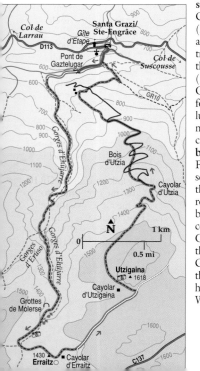

and Euskera. Head down the lane and, after a **bridge**, turn right at the first fork, following signs to the gorge. Turn right again, over a **second bridge** (5min; left is the GR10), then cross a **third bridge** (**Pont de Gaztelugar**), where the asphalt ends. Continue along a track which leads to the start of the **Gorges d'Ehüjarre** (**15min**).

Cross the stile to the left and follow the narrow path through lush vegetation reminiscent of more tropical climes, until it crosses the (probably) dry **river bed** for the first time (**30min**). From here we re-cross the river several times, steadily climbing up the middle of the gorge, until reaching a point where the two branches of river and gorge converge (1000m; **1h30min**). Cross to the left, to continue up the increasingly narrow Ehüjarre Gorge, leaving the Eruso Gorge to the right. The path keeps quite high above the river.

We emerge from the forest and

Above the cave in the Ehüjarre Gorge

climb the hillside to the **Grottes de Molerse** (**2h20min**), a couple of small caves inside the canyon wall — an ideal place to rest and contemplate the awesome views. The path continues to follow the left bank of the stream up onto the open mountain, passes a beautiful **waterfall** (**2h30min**) and then rounds the side of a second **waterfall,** to come out onto the open mountain with views ahead to Mt Lakora and other peaks straddling the border (**2h45min**). Continue briefly alongside the stream and cross it, following signs and waymarking up to the flat meadowlands of **Erraitz** (1430m; **3h**).

Follow the sign indicating SAINTE-ENGRACE PAR BOIS D'UTZIA and, keeping to the left of a **sheepfold** before the **Cayolar d'Erraitz**, look for waymarking on the rocks to guide you steeply up the mountainside. When you join a track (**3h20min**), follow it to the left and enter a forest, re-emerging on the mountainside by a **large rock** (**3h35min**). From here your path forks left, away from the track, to pass the ruined **Cayolar d'Utzigaina** and ascend gradually around the west side of **Mt Utzigaina** (1618m). There are fine views back towards the Pic d'Anie and the Larra karst area, as well as the upper reaches of the canyon where you have just walked.

From the highest point of the path (1550m; **3h50min**), we start a dizzying descent to the lower part of the canyon and the Santa Grazi valley and church. Our first landmark is the **Cayolar d'Utzia** (**4h40min**), at the entrance to the **Bois d'Utzia**. Entering this forest on a track (which you *could* follow all the way down to Santa Grazi, although this would be extremely tedious), fork left on a **path** (**4h45min**). This is the first of several short cuts down through the forest (keep your eyes peeled for green/white/yellow waymarking on trees). It rejoins the track on a sharp bend, from where the canyon entrance is visible (**5h25min**).

From here we have no choice but to follow this track downhill for 15 minutes — until we reach another waymarked path leading left alongside a **drystone wall** (**5h40min**). This brings us to a collection of old **farm buildings** (**5h50min**), from where we turn sharp right along a narrow, fairly overgrown path between fields, crossing the track again to eventually link up with the GR10 (**6h**). Cross the river bridge to return to the junction with your outward route, and walk up the lane, back to the **church** at **Santa Grazi/Ste-Engrâce** (**6h15min**).

Walk 32: COL DE LA PIERRE-ST MARTIN • COL D'ARLAS • ARLAS • COL DE PESCAMOU • ARLAS VALLEY • COL DE LA PIERRE-ST MARTIN

Distance: 5.6km; 3.5mi; 2h25min
Grade: short but strenuous, with an ascent of 365m. The final section, to the summit and back, is steep but safe. Although short, this is the only walk in this book which exceeds an altitude of 2000m and so should only be attempted in clear weather — especially the return route through the karst labyrinth of Larra, where there is considerable risk of getting lost. Note that there is likely to be snow at this altitude from December to April. The only waymarking (faded yellow paint) is from the starting point to Col d'Arlas, although on a clear day the rest of the route is fairly obvious.

Equipment: see page 55
Access: 🚗 Follow Car tour 8 to the **Col de Soudet** (1540m; 75km), and turn right towards *PIERRE-ST MARTIN* on the D132. Turn right just before this small ski resort towards *ISABA* and the border, to the **Col de la Pierre-St Martin** (1765m), the French/Spanish border. Park on the left, by an old refuge (a 3.5km detour from the Col de Soudet). The Refugio de Belagua, 7km below the col on the Spanish side (tel. 948 394002), offers meals and accommodation and makes a good base for exploring the area.

An ascent of Arlas provides a relatively easy and short way to reach a 2000m-high Pyrenean peak and enjoy superb views over the unique karst area of Larra — as well as towards neighbouring higher mountains such as the Pic d'Anie. The return walk, provided the weather is clear, is a beautiful amble through the Arlas valley, which is one of the more accessible parts of Larra, a labyrinth of limestone rock formations and Spanish pine.

From the parking area at the **Col de la Pierre-St Martin**, cross the road to peer down into the seemingly bottomless abyss marking the entrance to the San Martin cave complex, one of the largest in Europe. Then **start the walk:** look for a path which starts behind the **old refuge** and, with the pointed peak of Arlas clearly visible ahead to the left, follow this path over pastureland and between rocks, to descend to a small **pond** (**10min**). From here follow yellow waymarking on rocks and cairns,

to rise steadily up the hillside to the base of the mountain. Then *leave* the main path and the way-marking (which veers to the right; **25min**); instead head left to the **Col d'Arlas** (**30min**). From here follow a narrow path round the north side of the mountain and then steeply to the summit of **Arlas** (2043m; **50min**). Below to the north is the ugly development of the Arette-la-Pierre-St Martin ski resort, but to the east and south is the extraordinary karst spectacle of Larra — its focal point is the abrupt north face of Pic d'Anie.

From the summit, watch your step as you descend steeply down the narrow ridge path on the opposite side of the mountain. When you reach a cairn marking the grassy **Col de Pescamou** (1918m; **1h10min**, pinpoint a pond to the south, at the beginning of the **Arlas valley**, and simply follow the gully (there is no real path) down to the meadowland and the **pond** (**1h30min**).

Beyond the pond, follow the vestiges of a path, meandering through this karst landscape interspersed with Spanish pine. Fortunately, the larger hollows in the valley are fenced off, but you still need to exercise a little caution. If you lose the path, there is no problem, as long as you keep heading down this narrow valley; You will soon join another path and eventually come to a road (**2h05min**) — at the point where it makes a 360° loop. You are now about 1.5km inside the Spanish border. Follow the road back uphill and over the bridge, to return to your starting point at the **Col de la Pierre-St Martin** (**2h25min**).

At the start of the walk, with the Pic d'Anie in the background

● Index

Geographical names comprise the only entries in this index; for other subjects, see Contents on page 3. **Bold face** type indicates a photograph; *italic type* indicates a map (both may be in addition to other entries on the same page).

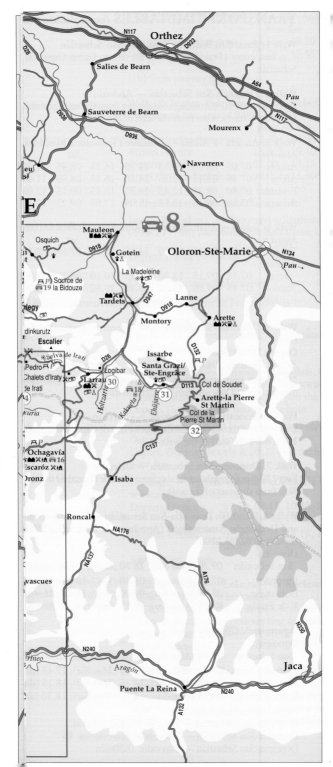

Pamplona — Orbaitzeta (Autobuses Rio Irati; (948 303570)

	Mon-Fri	Sat
amplona	19.00	13.30
ta	07.00 (Mon-Sat)	

ximately 1h

-de-Luz — Ascain — Col Ste-Engrâce* (Autocars le Basque (59262587)

	Mon/Tue/Thu/Fri			Wed	
e-Luz	11.30	14.00	17.30	13.15	19.00
	08.00	13.35	18.55	08.00	15.50

days	Mon-Sat		
e-Luz	10.30	14.15	19.00
	08.50	13.35	18.30

to Col St Ignace (for the Larrun funicular railway, 10min past
Sara/Sare and its caves (20 and 35 min past Ascain respectively)

ne/Baiona — Itxassou (train; www.ter-sncf.com)

| ayonne | 18.03 | Departs Itxassou | 07.30 |
| | 18.34 | Arrives Baiona/Bayonne | 08.02 |

ne/Baiona — Bidarrai (train; www.ter-sncf.com)

ayonne	08.55	11.24	18.03		
	09.32	12.01	18.46		
	07.18	10.24	13.51	17.14	19.11
ayonne	08.08	11.01	14.28	17.51	19.48

an-de-Luz — Cambo — Urcuray/Urkoi — Hazparren ata, (0559 541137)

	Tue-Fri	Wed	Mon/Tue/Thu/Fri
e-Luz	11.00	13.05	17.30
Jrkoi	11.45	14.00	18.25

	Mon-Fri	Tue/Fri
Urkoi	07.05	13.40
-Luz	07.55	14.30

ys			
e-Luz	11.00	Departs Urcuray/Urkoi	19.10
Jrkoi	11.50	Arrives St Jean-de-Luz	20.00

lic transport

lic transport

lic transport